The Book of
Cheiro's St

"In working ~~through~~ ~~this book~~
~~p~~ages, I have carefully ~~investigated~~ ~~every~~
i~~m~~portant form of occultism whether it has been
Hindus, Egyptian, Chaldean or Greek... The
purpose of this book is to endeavour to show in a
clear and simple manner the useful and practical
truth that underlies the so called occult study of
reading character and disposition by the 'period
of birth'. There is not a rule that I have given
concerning character, tendencies or health, which
has not been thoroughly verified by me in my
own work".

Cheiro
From the Preface

"If astrology, palmistry or numerology can help us
understand ourselves better, we will surely be able to
conduct our lives in a more orderly level.... to have
more understanding and compassion towards others
and accept them as they are".

Jagjit Uppal

The Book of the Zodiac

Cheiro's

STUDY OF YOUR PERIOD OF BIRTH

ORIENT PAPERBACKS
A Divison of Vision Books Pvt. Ltd.
New Delhi • Mumbai • Hyderabad

*Based on the original writings of Count
Louis Hamon 'Cheiro'. Adapted by the editors.*

ISBN 81-222-0317-5

1st Published in Orient Paperbacks 2002

*The Book of the Zodiac:
Cheiro's Study of Your Period of Birth*

© Vision Books Pvt. Ltd.

Cover design by Vision Studio

Published by
Orient Paperbacks
(A division of Vision Books Pvt. Ltd.)
Madarsa Road, Kashmere Gate, Delhi-110 006

Printed in India at
Rakesh Press, Delhi-110 028

Cover Printed at
Ravindra Printing Press, Delhi-110 006

PREFACE

The purpose of this book is to endeavour to show in a clear and simple manner the useful and practical truth that underlies the so-called occult study of reading character and disposition by the "period of birth", and the meaning of the number of each day and the influence of such things on human life. It will, I hope, be seen in reading these pages how perfect is the mechanism of the Universe, by which certain characteristics, and even details as to health, may be traced by a study of such things.

Many books have been published that pretend to deal with these questions, and although some of these books may be excellent in their own way, I have found that, as a rule, they have been too complicated in their method or too involved in their theories to be of *practical use* to the everyday man or woman who has not had the occult training necessary to understand complicated expositions on such subjects.

I have been encouraged to send this work on its way by the great success which has attended the publication of other works from my pen on the Study of the Hand, and the commendation I have received for the "faculty of expressing myself clearly, and in simple language", making the studies of practical use and help to a wider range of people than books of this class usually reach.

In the present book I have drawn largely from my own experiences in this study of character, and I may safely state that *there is not a rule I have given concerning character tendencies or health, which has not been thoroughly verified by me in my own work, which has extended in a professional way over a period of more than forty years.*

Considering that during this period I was consulted on an average by from fifteen to twenty persons a day, I think I may safely claim to have had a wider field in which to gather the knowledge necessary for this book than, perhaps, any other writer on this subject.

I have seen so many wrecked and broken lives, where, had the people possessed even a slight knowledge of their own dispositions, they might have been saved, that I have felt it a duty to publish in a cheap and simple form the indications of character and tendencies which may be easily learned by a study of these "periods of birth", as set forth in the following pages.

I believe that any aid that may help towards the observation of character is *not only useful but even essential if one wishes to keep abreast and succeed in this age of ever-increasing competition.*

Those people who have some means at their command to learn their own characters and the dispositions of others must certainly be thrice armed in the battle of life, and consequently more successful than the people who know nothing of such things. Therefore I have no hesitation in saying that with this book in one's possession, one has a means towards winning success and also happiness.

With even a slight knowledge of what I designate in these pages as Life's Natural Affinities, the road to the divorce courts would not be so crowded as it is at present, parents would more easily understand their children and children their parents, and a great deal of suffering and friction might be avoided.

In conclusion, I trust I am not presuming too much when I venture to hope that this unpretentious volume may be the means of helping a large proportion of my fellow-beings to realise that in the study of the mysteries of life we are giving praise and glory to the Creator of Life, who in His infinite wisdom created all things to be used by man for the highest development of his kind.

CHEIRO

CONTENTS

LIST OF ILLUSTRATIONS

It will be my effort all through these pages, to write as clearly and simply as possible, keeping before my mind that the teacher has at one time been the pupil, and that the pupil of today may be the teacher of tomorrow. From the innumerable letters I have received, I have learned that the great number of people desire to have put before them as much information as possible on the influence of the Zodiac on human life, its effect on character, its causation of difficulties between men and women, with the other hundred and one tendencies it calls into being.

CHEIRO

THE ZODIAC

The Zodiac is the most important element in our study of Astrology and of the significance of the date of birth in a person's life and destiny. It is an imaginary circle around the Earth. This imaginary circle is the apparent passage of the

The word Zodiac is derived from the Greek word *zôè* meaning "life", and from *diabos* which means "wheel". Hence the word zodiac can be translated as the "wheel of life".

The word *zôè* is etymologically linked to *zôon*, which means animal, and the Zodiac has often been called "The Path of the Animals". Eight of the twelve signs actually represent animals.

Sun, as seen from the Earth, as it traverses from 'day to night, sunrise to sunset', throughout the year. Actually this passage of the Sun is caused by the Earth's movement around the Sun.

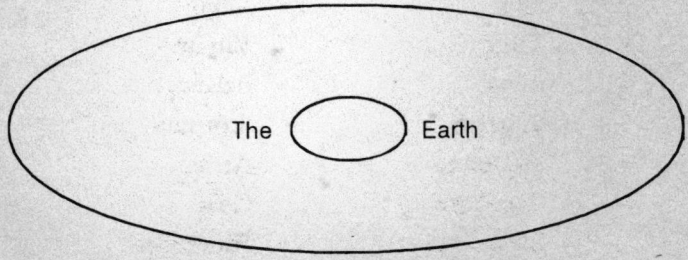

Fig. I
The Ecliptic: The imaginary path of the
Sun around the Earth.

The apparent path which the Sun seems to take is circular in shape and is called ecliptic. All planets of the solar system also confine their lateral movement along this path or the track. This broad belt extending about 9° on either side of the ecliptic is known as the Zodiac.

The Zodiac, as explained, is circular in shape and therefore, has 360°. For astrological purposes, the ecliptic or Sun's annual path is divided into twelve equal parts. Each of the twelve equal parts contains 30°. These twelve equal parts are represented by imaginary figures or signs. These signs are not bodies but spaces of thirty degrees and divide the ecliptic, or the apparent track of the Sun (and planets) round the earth into twelve equal parts. These 12 divisions are called the 'Signs of the Zodiac'.

Thus we have 12 Zodiac signs one for each of the 12 parts. They are:

Zodiac Sign	Represented by
Aries	Ram
Taurus	Bull
Gemini	Twins
Cancer	Crab
Leo	Lion
Virgo	Virgin
Libra	Balance
Scorpio	Scorpion
Sagittarius	Archer
Capricorn	Goat
Aquarius	Waterman
Pisces	Fishes

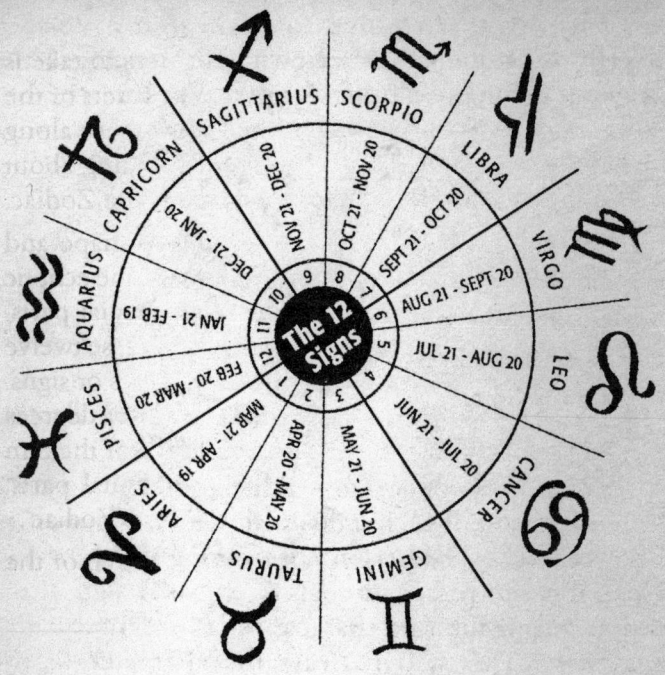

Fig. II : The Zodiac Signs

We now come to a very important part of our study, in which we shall consider the Sun's apparent passage through the twelve signs of the Zodiac, caused by the earth's movement around the Sun. On the basis of the 12 divisions of the Zodiac, the Greeks, as geometers and mathematicians, developed a calender during fifth century B.C. Each of the Zodiac signs was assigned to represent a set of days (dates) in a year. A person born between those dates is said to be born under that particular Zodiac sign.

Astrology attributes to each sign a certain specialised influence of its own. The nature of the influence is obtained from its ruler or its lord.

Signs	Ruling Planets
Leo	Sun
Cancer	Moon
Aries, Scorpio	Mars
Gemini, Virgo	Mercury
Sagittarius, Pisces	Jupiter
Taurus, Libra	Venus
Capricorn, Aquarius	Saturn

From the Sun's position each month we may judge of the character of each individual. We shall learn that, more or less, every person born during the period in which the Sun passes through a particular sign of the Zodiac will exhibit its characterisitcs as delineated in this study. This will indicate the character of the Individual then born, and by the same rule when the Moon is found in these signs at birth the Personality will be described.

The Cusp

Since the Zodiac is circular in shape, each sign is under the influence of its previous sign and the incoming sign for a period of seven days. These junction points of the houses are called the "cusp" of the houses. For example the Zodiacal sign of Capricorn commences on December 21, but for seven days, it is overlapped by the "cusp" of the previous sign—Sagittarius. It does not come into its full strength until or about December 28. From this date onwards it is in full strength until January

20, and is then for seven days gradually losing its strength on account of being overlapped by the "cusp" of the incoming sign — Aquarius.

So, each sign has two "cusp" periods during which its influence is diminished because of its preceding and succeeding signs.

The Elements

The twelve Zodiacal signs are also divided into four groups, representing the four basic elements—Fire, Earth, Air and Water. Each of the elements rules three signs. Thus the signs, starting from Aries onwards, are termed sequentially as Fiery, Earthy, Airy and Watery.

Fiery	*Earthy*	*Airy*	*Watery*
Aries	Taurus	Gemini	Cancer
Leo	Virgo	Libra	Scorpio
Sagittarius	Capricorn	Aquarius	Pisces

Each group of three signs is called 'Triplicity'. The practical significance of this division of the sign into elements will fully be understood later in this book.

Generally people born under Fire signs are enthusiastic, energetic and optimistic. People of Earth signs are practical, down to earth and realistic. People born under Air signs are intellectuals and thinkers, whereas people of Water signs are of emotional nature. They are also sensitive and intuitive.

My interest is in the future because I am going to spend the rest of my life there.

Charles F Kettsing

JANUARY

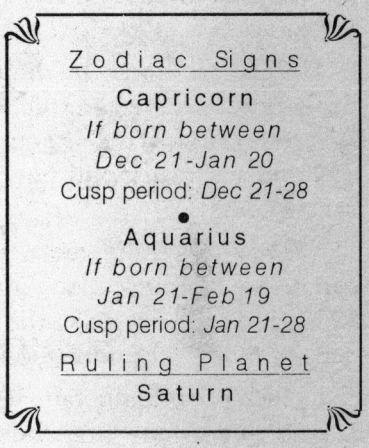

The Zodiacal Sign of
Capricorn
commences on
December 21, but for
seven days, being
overlapped by the
"cusp" of the previous
sign — Sagittarius, it
does not come into its
full power until on or
about December 28. From this date onwards it is in
full strength until January 20, and is then for seven
days gradually losing its strength on account of becoming
overlapped by the "cusp" of the incoming sign —
Aquarius.

Zodiac Signs
Capricorn
If born between
Dec 21-Jan 20
Cusp period: *Dec 21-28*
●
Aquarius
If born between
Jan 21-Feb 19
Cusp period: *Jan 21-28*
Ruling Planet
Saturn

People born between January 20 and 27, partake
of the characteristics of both Capricorn and Aquarius,
and the same rule applies to all those born within the
"cusp" of any sign.

Personality Traits

People born in this period have a deep devotional
nature, and make great efforts to do good to others, but
generally to masses of people rather than to individual.
Although they appear cold, they have warm hearts

towards suffering, and as a rule they give largely to charities.

If inclined to be religious they usually go to extremes, and become fanatical in their zeal. They worship intellectual, clever people, and are deep thinkers.

They are quick in their intuition of people and things but they are as a rule, too easily discouraged and lack self-confidence. They rarely interfere with the affairs of others, but they will never stand interference from others too.

They generally make their greatest mistake by espousing an unpopular cause, the "under dog" in the fight, and so often make the bitterest enemies by their actions being misunderstood.

Such people generally feel their responsibilities too keenly, and often worry themselves into bad health.

On Being Successful

These people are independent and high-minded in all their actions and detest being under the restraint of others.

They often make excellent speakers, but not so much through oratory as by "plain speaking;" they "hit straight from the shoulder," and go direct to the point of the subject in plain language. Infact they are thinkers, reasoners and make natural heads of business organisations or any form of government work. They must be leaders in whatever they are engaged, or else they are inclined to lose their interest in their work. They should aim for some form of public life, and in such careers they generally do best such as in the government and in responsible positions of control and management of others.

Friends and Relationships

People born in this period usually make the most solid and best friendships with people who are born in their own period viz., between December 21 to end of January, from April 20 to the end of May, and with their "central affinities," June 21 to July 20-27, and August 21 to September 20-27 (See Fig. VII, Page 113).

These people have strong mental force, but they are, as a rule, generally misunderstood by others. They have strange ideas of love, duty and social position, and for this reason they are often considered "odd," and do not fit in easily with their neighbours. They are inclined to excite bitter opposition but bear up against it with a philosophic spirit. Their home and family life is very often a troubled one. They usually have distressed or invalid relatives to look after and as a rule they sacrifice themselves to home interests. They feel "lonely hearted" and misunderstood.

Health

The influence of Saturn on those born in January indicates a vigorous constitution and good physical stamina. At the same time there is a strong tendency to depression and despondency which if not acted against will induce bilous attacks, trouble with the gall bladder, ulcers in the stomach, deragements of digestive organs and stoppages of the intestines. As a rule these people are more inclined to suffer from rheumatism and gout, pains in the feet, and hurts and accidents to the legs and ankles, troubles with the spleen and lever, ruptures, decay of the teeth, and pains in the teeth and ears.

Cold seriously affects these persons. They are likely to suffer from asthma, bronchial catarrh and such like ailments. High dry climates suit them better than living in low altitudes. They need to study well their diet and keep up the circulation by adequate exercise, also avoid draughts, damp and cold winds. All kinds of skin diseases do happen to them. This part of Zodiac has a kind of sub-rule over the stomach, they often suffer from vomiting and nausea. If their outlook should ever become limited or cramped, and conditions show signs of giving way, their innate gloom may turn to hypochondria unless they exert every force of their nature to cultivate the spirit of cheerfulness.

Finance

The dominant influence of Saturn ruling the birth-month is not a favourable significator for those born in January, as it causes delays, hindrances and limitations in regard to financial advancement, at least in the early part of the life.

Advancement, gain and success in money is promised by industry, perseverance and by carefulness, thrift and economy. Infact, these people acquire wealth through their own personal efforts than by any dint of good fortune. Advantageous investments for them would be in land or house property, the building up of factories dealing especially in coal, lead or iron products, machinery for transport work or agriculture, the developing of farming enterprises and all things solid and concrete.

They should never lend money without security, or they would be sure to lose. Investment of money should be entirely based on the solid foundations of the concerns.

Colours

The colours which give the most suitable vibrations to persons born in this period, and which are the most beneficial to them, are all tones of grey, all ranges of violet, purple and black.

Stones

The birth stones for this period are moon-stones, pearls and amethysts.

Various Concerns, Occasions, Undertakings, Activities and Interests Which Fall Under the Ruling Planet

Saturn: Deep study, concentration, exact and just reasoning, mining, dealing in property and real estate, farming and gardening, drawing, mathematics, occasions requiring an absolutely balanced and unemotional state of mind.

Some Famous Persons
Born in this Part of the Year

Marilyn Monroe	1
Clement Attlee	3
Sir Issac Pitman	4
Zulfikar Ali Bhutto	5
Mansur Ali Khan Pataudi	5
Kapil Dev	6
Joan of Arc	6
Vijay Tendulkar	7
Elvis Presley	8
Richard Nixon	9
Lord Curzon	11
Swami Vivekanand	12
N A Palkhivala	16
Benjamin Franklin	17
Lord Byron (Poet)	22
Francis Bacon (Philosopher)	22
Subhash Chandra Bose	23
Frederick the Great of Prussia	24
Somerset Maughm (Writer)	25
Gen K M Cariappa	28
Lala Lajpat Rai	28
Franklin D Roosevelt	30
Norman Mailer	31

FEBRUARY

┌─────────────────────────────┐
│ **Zodiac Signs** │
│ **Aquarius** │
│ *If born between* │
│ *Jan 21-Feb 19* │
│ Cusp period: *Jan 21- 28* │
│ • │
│ **Pisces** │
│ *If born between* │
│ *Feb 20-March 20* │
│ Cusp period: *Feb 20-27* │
│ **Ruling Planets** │
│ Saturn *for* Aquarius │
│ Jupiter *for* Pisces │
└─────────────────────────────┘

The Zodiacal Sign of Aquarius commences on January 21, but for seven days, being overlapped by the "cusp" of the previous sign — Capricorn, it does not come into full power until on or about January 28. From this date onwards it is in full strength until February 19. It is then for seven days gradually losing its strength on account of becoming overlapped by the "cusp" of the incoming sign — Pisces.

Those born in the "cusp" take from the qualities of both signs.

Personality Traits

People born in this period are generally over-sensitive. They feel very lonely in life and are easily wounded in their feelings. They are usually high-strung, and their nerves are generally over-wrought; they often lose control of themselves, and say or do things that they bitterly regret later. They read character instinctively, and for this reason they "see through" people too easily to be really happy.

They are generally very active for the public good, and will often give all they have to relieve the distress of others. They take a great interest in public meetings, gatherings of people and public ceremonies. They love theatres and concerts, and like to be where crowds of people congregate, and yet they always have the feelings that they are alone in life.

On Being Successful

People born in this part of the year are generally good reasoners, and are very successful in debate and argument, and difficult to convince. They genrally have a scientific turn of mind especially in relation to inventions dealing with electricity or such like things.

They are excellent in business and finance when they apply their minds to such things, but as a general rule they are more successful for others, and make more money for others than for themselves.

They require some call of duty or circumstance to show the qualities that are in them. If "the call" does come they often rise to great things, but if it does not come, they wait often until it is too late to develop their great qualities.

If people born under this sign overcome their sensitiveness and develop their will-power, there is no position in life they could not attain. They generally succeed best in some large sphere of action, where they can feel their responsibilities for others. Those who are "awakened" usually leave a great name behind. They have "visions" and imagination.

They generally possess the controlling powers in their eyes which subdue others.

Their greatest fault is that it generally takes some sudden call of circumstances to "make the most of themselves."

If born with money, these people rarely show what is in them. They are inclined in ordinary conditons to let their opportunities slip, or realise them only when it is too late. If, however, people born in this period belong to the lower order of humanity, they lose all sense of honour and principle, and are extremely unreliable, tricky in money matters, dishonest, and unscrupulous in gaining what they desire.

Friends and Realtionships

In real friendship or love people born in this period get on very well with those born from May 21 to June 20-27 and from September 21 to October 20-27 and also with those born in November 20-27, or with those born in the centre of the triangle. (See Fig. VI, Page 112).

They are not demonstrative in affection, but feel very deeply. If they "like" they fight to the bitter end for their friend; but if they dislike they are just as intense, and if they belong to the lower plane of humanity they will stick at nothing to avenge an injury or what they feel to be an injustice.

Health

These people are inclined to suffer most from the stomach, often through the nerves of the stomach in some peculiar manner that is difficult to relieve with ordinary medicine. If care is not taken they are inclined to suffer from the bladder, kidneys and swellings or dropsy in the legs.

Bad circulation of the blood and cold hands and feet also generally trouble them. Attacks of jaundice are inclined to affect them.

They are also prone to suffer from accidents to their teeth, pains in the knees and middle of the spine, and breaks or sprains of the feet and ankles, and often some delicacy of the eyes.

Finance

The influence of Saturn and Uranus governing this part of the Zodiac gives the likelihood of great and sudden changes in the fortunes. People born in this month are liable to experience remarkable and unexpected reversals and they should be very careful in matters of an uncertain or hazardous nature. It is a favourable position however, for them receiving an income from trusts, insurance companies, banking concerns, railway companies, electrical installations, aviation and through floating of inventions.

Unless they are extremely prudent, their income, however, will always be more or less uncertain. At some period of their lives, they are likely to come into a great deal of money from a totally unlooked for source.

Colours

The most favourable colours for them are all shades of what are known as "electric shades," as electric blues and electric greys. These are the foundation colours for people born during this period.

Stones

The birth stones for this period are sapphires, pink topazes, and moonstones.

Various Concerns, Occasions, Undertakings, Activities and Interests Which Fall Under the Ruling Planets

Saturn: Deep study, concentration, exact and just reasoning, mining, dealing in property and real estate, farming and gardening, drawing, mathematics, occasions requiring an absolutely balanced and unemotional state of mind.

Jupiter: Business and trading of every kind, investments, ceremonies and functions, seeking favour, settlements in litigation, ceremonial and philanthropic occasions of every kind where it is desired to help others and incidentally help one's self.

Some Famous Persons
Born in This Part of the Year

MARCH

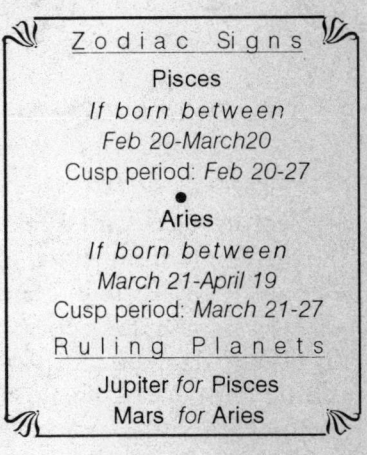

Zodiac Signs

Pisces
If born between
Feb 20-March20
Cusp period: *Feb 20-27*

•

Aries
If born between
March 21-April 19
Cusp period: *March 21-27*

Ruling Planets

Jupiter *for* Pisces
Mars *for* Aries

The Zodiacal Sign of Pisces commences on February 20, but for seven days, being overlapped by the "cusp" of the previous sign — Aquarius, it does not come into its full power until about February 27. From this date onwards it is in full strength until March 20, and it is then for seven days gradually losing its strength on account of becoming overlapped by the "cusp" of the incoming sign — Aries.

Personality Traits

Although by nature generous, people born in this period are usually over-anxious about money matters, and inclined to worry about what their future position in life may be. This state of mind is, I think, largely due to their dislike and dread of being dependent on others more than from any love of money.

This quality makes them, however, much misunderstood, and they are often considered close in money matters when in reality they are not.

People born in this period often go back on thier promises, especially on questions of money. They promise to give, on the impulse of the moment, but if they have time for reflection then the fear of future poverty forces them, as a rule, to break their promise or give, perhaps, only one half of what they had stipulated.

They are inclined to brood and to melancholy, or to imagine all the world is against them and that they are being made martyrs of.

The strongest and weakest characters are found in this sign. Some are inclined to gratify their innate sense of luxury and self-indulgence and, if this side of the nature is the one that controls, they are likely to be too easy going, to be too receptive to their surroundings, to become influenced by false friends, to give way to fraudulent schemes and in some cases are inclined to become addicted to drugs or drink.

If, however, persons born in this part of the year find some purpose worth living for, they rise to the emergency as no others can. These are the people that one meets sometimes in life who surprise their friends by their sudden change of character.

They can, in a moment, throw off any form of weakness or self-indulgence, and rise to any height of self-denial. All persons born in this part of the year have a dual element as the mainspring of their nature. It simply depends on which of the two roads they have decided to follow.

People born in this period are highly emotional. If they belong to the weak side of it, they are easily influenced by the people with whom they are thrown into contact, but if they belong to the stronger side, their emotional nature can lift them up to any height.

They are generally fond of the sea and large expanses of water. If circumstances do not permit them to travel, they will, if they possibly can, make their homes where they can see the ocean, or on the side of some lake, or river.

Almost all have a curiously mystical side to their nature as well as the practical. They are often classed as superstitious, the occult in all its forms appealing to them in one way or another.

They love to search out or investigate the unknown, the philosophical, or the mysterious. Although by nature generous, they have at heart a curious dread of poverty, and for that reason do not allow their generous instincts to get the better of them, unless they are under the influence of someone they love. In such a case they become easily influenced and are as likely as not to give away all they possess.

They require some call of duty or circumstances to show the qualities that are in them. If "the call" does come, they often rise to great things, but if it does not come, they wait often until it is too late to develop their great qualities.

On Being Successful

These people possess a curiously "natural understanding," which they donot obtain from books or study. They easily acquire, or rather absorb knowledge, especially of the history of countries, travel, research, and like subjects.

These people are also more mentally ambitious than otherwise. They may know their subject well in their mind, but they will hesitate and undervalue their own individuality if they find they have to put it to a test in any public manner.

They have great fidelity and loyalty if trust is imposed on them, and great persistence in carrying out whatever work they have in their hands to perform, and they are generally found in positions of trust and responsibility for others.

Many artists, musicians and literary people are born in this period, but they must receive great encouragement ever to make the best of themselves.

They have great loyalty to friends or to any cause they take up, provided they feel they are trusted or looked up to. They are generally successful in all positions of responsibility, but at the same time they are not inclined to push themselves forward, and usually "wait to be asked" before giving their opinions.

They are great respectors of "law and order," and uphold the conventions of whatever the social order in which they may be found.

In business they are good in dealing with shipping, trade with foreign countries, or sea-borne commerce of any description.

Sea captains, sailors of all kinds, also travellers are often found under this sign.

Money has no value in their eyes. It is simply something to be used and nothing more.

If people born in this sign overcome their sensitiveness and develop their will-power, there is no position in life they could not attain. They generally succeed best in some large sphere of action, where they can feel their responsibilities for others. Those who are "awakened" in this sign usually leave a great name behind. They have "visions" and imagination.

Friends and Relationships

They will find their more lasting friendships and affections with those born in their own period or between June 21 and July 20 and on account of "the cusp" to about the end of the month; and with their "central affinities", August 21 to September 20-27, also October 21 to November 20-27. (See Fig. V, Page 111).

People born in this period have great loyalty to friends or to any cause they take up, provided they feel they are trusted or looked up to. They are highly emotional. If they belong to the weak side of it, they are easily influenced by the people with whom they are thrown in contact, but if they belong to the stronger side, their emotional nature can lift them upto any position. Although they have a strong love of home and home ties, they often find themselves at variance with members of their family. They make friends easily with those in high positions, but with those in their own sphere or beneath , they will be prone to make many bitter enemies.

Health

People born in this period are mostly inclined to suffer from nerves, insomnia, disorder of the blood, poor circulation and anaemia. Though being over-anxious, they often bring on despondency and melancholy which impairs the digestive organs, inclining them to nervous disorders and in many cases to paralysis. They often suffer from intestinal trouble, pain in the feet and head, and are disposed to rheumatism. They are more inclined to get attacks of consumption. The skin of the body exudes perspiration easily, especially the hands and feet. They should, if possible, live in bright, sunny, dry climates, and take a great amount of fresh air and exercise. They are fond of travel, are restless, and love to be continually on the move.

Finance

Jupiter in this part of the year is in its negative House in the Zodiac, it is more the mental side of the ambitions that are called into being. Persons born in this period will consequently be more ambitious mentally than physically. They often dream great dreams of what they want or expect themselves to be and often lack of purpose or physical effort to achieve their results. It is , in consequence, what might be called an uncertain sign for finance and many "ups and downs" of fortune will threaten persons born in this period unless they have schooled themselves to follow out their ambitions to a climax.

They are however, more or less careless in money matters and are not inclined to save up for a "rainy day". They are often found to "waste their substance" and face poverty and loss of position in their advancing years.

Colours

The colours most suitable to them are all shades of mauve, violet, and purple. These are the foundation colours of this period.

Stones

The birth stones for this period are agates, sapphires, amethysts, and emeralds.

Various Concerns, Occasions, Undertakings, Activities and Interests Which Fall Under the Ruling Planets

Jupiter: Business and trading of every kind, investments, ceremonies and functions, seeking favour, settlements in litigation, ceremonial and philanthropic occasions of every kind where it is desired to help others and incidentally help one's self.

Mars: Sports, games, hunting, fighting, wrestling, all that requires force, and strong and prompt action: mechanical work, "stunting", surgery, public agitations and movements.

Some Famous Persons
Born in this Part of the Year

APRIL

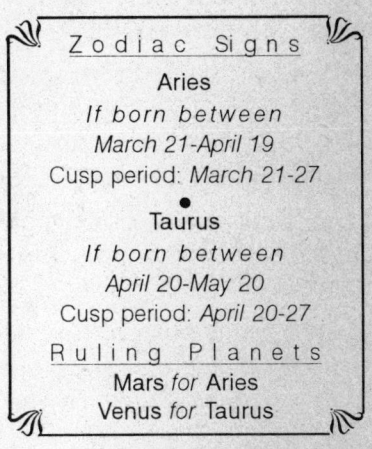

The Zodiacal Sign of Aries commences on March 21, but for seven days, being overlapped by the "cusp" of the previous sign — Pisces, it does not come into its full power until about March 27. From this date onwards, it is in full strength until April 19. It is then for seven days gradually losing its strength on account of becoming overlapped by the "cusp" of the incoming sign — Taurus.

Personality Traits

People born in this period are endowed with great mental energy, full of new schemes and original plans for anything they are interested in. They are self-willed, and nothing but hard facts and reason will make them see things in any light but their own.

They are inclined to lack caution, being by nature impulsive and quick in thought and action.

They go to extremes in all things, are frank and outspoken, and inclined to make enemies by want of tact.

The lower type of this sign will stick at nothing to accomplish their purpose. As masters they are brutal and tyrannical and often meet a violent death. The higher type are good masters but at the same time severe in discipline and more or less exacting in the service they expect from others.

Both classes have a distinct desire to peer into the future, perhaps because they are impatient for things to develop. They are inclined to prophesy what will take place, and are often very gifted in this direction.

They desire to be looked up to and regarded as the "head" in their homes, in their business, and in their careers.

Persons born in this sign seldom get through life without receiving cuts, wounds, or blows to the head, either from accidents or violence.

On Being Successful

People born in this section of the year have unusually strong will power and great obstinacy of purpose.

They are born fighters in every sense of the word; they have also the greatest ability as organisers on a large scale, such as in the organisation of big schemes or as the heads of big business, and also in the organisation of armies or development of countries. They are enormously ambitious; as a rule they succeed in life and amass money and position.

They seem to resent all criticism, and the only way to offset this in them is by quiet logic, reason, and proof.

These people are intensely independent in work. They must do everything in their own way, and if they are interfered with by others they generally make a muddle of their plans or step back and let the other person take their place.

As far as material success or power is concerned, there are no heights to which persons born in this sign cannot climb — provided they "keep their heads." Success, however, is often their undoing, praise and flattery are inclined to make them have "swelled heads." In such conditions they do not "see straight," and by obstinate, arrogant actions, in many cases, they bring about their own ruin.

Friends and Relationships

They will find their more lasting friendships and affections with those born in their own period or between July 21 and August 20-27, and from November 21 to December 20-27; and also from the centre of their triangle, September 21 to October 20-27. (See Fig. IV, Page 109).

As a rule they are unhappy in their domestic life, for they rarely meet members of the opposite sex who understand them, and if opposition does not upset them from this point it usually does through their children.

Yet these people, be they men or women, crave for affection and sympathy more than anything else, and this is generally the rock on which they are finally wrecked if they have not the good fortune to meet their right affinities.

As a general rule, the men born in this part of the year suffer a great deal through their affections; they seldom understand women, and make great mistakes in their relations with them.

Health

People born in this period should try to obtain more sleep than almost any other class. They overwork their brains, and are inclined to suffer from all things that concern the head, — from headache, trouble with the eyes, inflammation of the brain; and there is often a tendency to apoplexy and rushes of blood to the head. They are also likely to have eruptions on the face and head, and trouble with the passages of the nose, such as polypi. And they are liable to get cuts and wounds in the head, and they usually run great danger from fire and explosions from engines, firearms, and machines generally. They seldom get through life without operations and a good deal of experience with the surgeon's knife.

They can not be too careful in their habits and should live quietly, never exceeding temperate limits. They will always be more or less liable to feverish or inflammatory troubles. They should take vigorous daily exercise in the open air and avoid taking alcohol or any exciting drugs.

Finance

People born in April, being governed by the planet Mars, have usually good learning ability but tend to have extravagant ideas in monetary matters. They can be very practical where the management of others is concerned, but there is a strong tendency to impulsive action in all important matters and they are apt to rush recklessly into any big financial scheme that presents itself to their choice. Owing to their innate lavishness and large ideas, they are often liable to sudden and heavy losses and fluctuation of fortune.

They are very determined in the acquisition of wealth, but they gain more by judicious investments, industry and business than by actual luck.

These people are much inclined to be involved in litigation and quarrels that promote law suits and in such matters, as a general rule, they are not fortunate.

Colours

The most harmonious colour for them is all shades of red, — crimson, rose, and pink, — but when ill all shades of blue and violet are the most soothing and beneficial to them.

Stones

The birth stones for this period are rubies, garnets, and bloodstones.

Various Concerns, Occasions, Undertakings, Activities and Interests Which Fall Under the Ruling Planets

Mars: Sports, games, hunting, fighting, wrestling, all that requires force, and strong and prompt action: mechanical work, "stunting", surgery, public agitations and movements.

Venus: Love, courtship, mating, marriage, art, music, decoration, dress, entertaining, holidays, dancing, gambling, peacemaking, pleasure of every kind, healing, social occasions of every kind, almsgiving.

Some Famous Persons
Born in this Part of the Year

Guru Tegh Bahadur	1
Bismark (German Statesman)	1
Harindranath Chattopadhyay	2
S H F J Manekshaw	3
Marlon Brando	3
Jagjivan Ram	5
Pandit Ravi Shankar	7
William Wordsworth	7
V I Lenin	10
Ramanathan Krishnan	11
S Venkatraghavan	12
Ustad Ali Akbar Khan	14
Charlie Chaplin	16
Sir John Franklin (Explorer)	16
Adolf Hitler	20
Antony Quinn	21
William Shakespeare	23
Oliver Cromwell	24
Sir Stafford Cripps	24
Sonal Mansingh	30

MAY

T he Zodiacal Sign of Taurus commences on April 20, but for seven days, being overlapped by the "cusp" of the previous sign — Aries, it does not come into its full power until on or about April 27. From this day

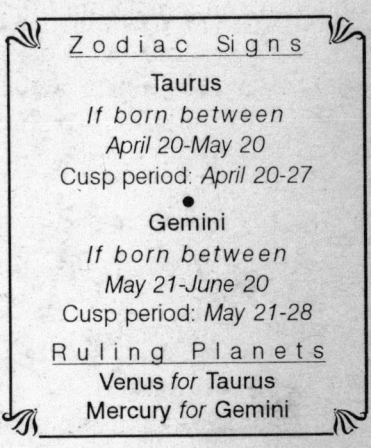

Zodiac Signs
Taurus
If born between
April 20-May 20
Cusp period: *April 20-27*
•
Gemini
If born between
May 21-June 20
Cusp period: *May 21-28*
Ruling Planets
Venus *for* Taurus
Mercury *for* Gemini

onwards it is in full strength until May 20, and is then for seven days gradually losing its strength on account of becoming overlapped by the "cusp" of the incoming sign — Gemini.

Personality Traits

People born in this section of the year have a curious power of dominating others, even when not conscious of trying to do so.

They have great power of endurance, both physical and mental, and can pass through enormous strains of fatigue as long as the excitement or determination lasts.

They generally tell the person they are going to fight with what they are going to do, and in consequence often get defeated at the commencement; but once their blood is roused they will go through every opposition until either one or the other is finished.

They are easily influenced by their surroundings, and become morbid and morose when trying to live under uncongenial conditions.

They should always decide all important questions when they are alone, for they seem to be so much in touch with the minds of those around them that they get confused, and often imagine other people's thoughts and ideas as their own. They are also too easily misled by their emotions, sensations, or affections.

They forgive at the slightest show of feeling or kindness, and this side of their nature makes them do all kinds of things that the world calls stupid.

On Being Successful

They have great ability to commit to memory from books, and are often very successful in literary work, but as a rule they love pleasure and society too much to make the best use of their gifts.

They make excellent directors, have good business intuition, but are generally considered richer than they really are, as they always dress well and look well.

As leaders in any case they inspire love and devotion, and often have great responsibility forced upon them.

They have an innate sense of harmony, rhythm and colour, and often succeed well in music, poetry and art, but, curiously enough, they usually lack the "money sense" to make the most of their qualities or talents.

Those born in this sign make excellent public servants, officials, or as heads in Government positions

48

or in the Army. They also make good, patient nurses and healers, and almost all have a keen love of gardening and flowers.

Friends and Relationships

They will find their most lasting friendships with people born between August 21-27, and September 20-27, December 21, and January 20-27, and with their "central affinities," October 21 to November 20-27. (See Fig. VII, Page 113).

These people are generally very unyielding in their determination, and are often called "stiff-necked" and obstinate, but when they love they are the most yielding and pliable of all, but only to those to whom they are attracted.

They are the most faithful and loyal friends. They are never happier than when entertaining their friends. They make wonderful hosts and hostesses, and have great taste about food.

They are governed by their sensations and by their loving nature; but affection has a greater hold on them than passion. If they love, they are generous to the last degree, and will consider no sacrifice too great for the person they care for, if they are enemies, they will fight with the most determined obstinacy to the death. But they always fight in the open, for they hate trickiness, double-dealing or deceit.

Neither men or women born in this period should marry early; their first marriage is usually a mistake.

As a rule both sexes are jealous in their disposition, and their jealousy often drives them into acts of violence or sudden exhibition of temper, which they bitterly regret when the storm is over.

Health

The influence of Venus on the people born in this period bestows on them abundance of vitality which should be guided into the proper channels and given out for the benefits of others, otherwise it is inclined to consume itself and develop morbid conditions. Although as a rule, these people are endowed with a splendid constitution, they suffer with all things that affect the throat, nasal cavities and upper part of the lungs. They are inclined to have inflammation of the throat, sore throat, diphtheria, polypus in the nose, and nasal catarrh.

As a rule their heart is more or less affected. They have fainting fits for no apparent reason, and often a tendency for "blood to the head," or apoplexy. Their flesh is easily bruised and they are liable to tumors and internal growths, especially if forced to live in damp places or wet climates.

Finance

This Zodiacal period of the year promises gain through cooperation, partnerships, associations as well as through marriage.

A strong desire to get money and possess wealth is one of the underlying qualities of the people born in this part of the year. This desire is actuated not so much from selfish reasons, but in order to be in a position to live well and help others.

For both sexes everything to do with the opening up, exploiting and developing of lands, mines and minerals, appears to be especially in their favour. Building schemes, even management of properties, such as hotels, restaurants and such like enterprises are also good and bring them success.

The women born in May generally marry in affluent families. They often exhibit considerable business ability and power of organization.

Colours

The colours most favourable to them are all shades of blue. Red is an exciting colour for them, and they should use it as little as possible.

Stones

The birth stones for this period are emeralds, turquoises, and lapis lazuli.

Various Concerns, Occasions, Undertakings, Activities and Interests Which Fall Under the Ruling Planets

Venus: Love, courtship, mating, marriage, art, music, decoration, dress, entertaining, holidays, dancing, gambling, peacemaking, pleasure of every kind, healing, social occasions of every kind, almsgiving.

Mercury: Travel, transport and communication of every kind: writing, television, radio, figuring, advertising, journalism, public speaking, education, and all things that concern the young.

Some Famous Persons
Born in this Part of the Year

Satayajit Ray	1
V. K. Krishna Menon	3
Audrey Hepburn	4
Thomas Huxley (Scientist)	4
Karl Marx	5
Rabindranath Tagore	6
Sigmund Freud	6
Robert Browning (Poet)	7
Harry S Truman	8
Florence Nightingale	12
Fahrenheit	14
Girish Karnad	19
Moshe Dayan	20
Christopher Columbus	20
P.T. Usha	20
Sir Arthur Conan Doyle (Writer)	22
Sir Laurence Oliver (Actor)	22
Thomas Hood (Poet)	23
Queen Victoria of England	24
Charles II	29

JUNE

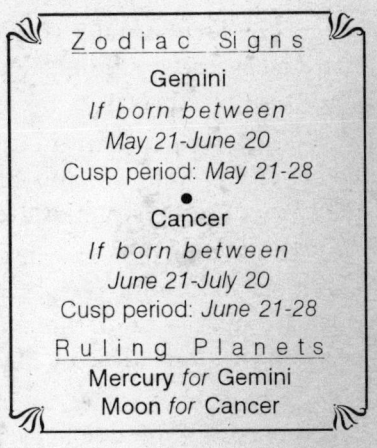

Zodiac Signs
Gemini
If born between
May 21-June 20
Cusp period: *May 21-28*
•
Cancer
If born between
June 21-July 20
Cusp period: *June 21-28*
Ruling Planets
Mercury *for* Gemini
Moon *for* Cancer

The Zodiacal Sign of Gemini — The Twins — commences on May 21, but for seven days, being overlapped by the "cusp" of the previous sign — Taurus, it does not come into its full power until on or about May 28. From this out it is in full strength until June 20, and is then for seven days gradually losing its strength on account of becoming overlapped by the "cusp" of the incoming sign — Cancer.

Persons born in this part of the year, namely, from May 21 to June 20, and in the "cusp" period from June 21 to June 27, have the characteristics of Gemini — The Twins — and are dual in character and in mentality.

Personality Traits

People born in this period are dual in character and mentality. The twin sides of their nature are perpetually pulling in opposite directions.

Their brains are subtle and brilliant, but they usually lack continuity of purpose.

Of all people they are the most difficult to understand; in temperament they are hot and cold almost at the same moment. They love with one side of their nature, and they are often critical and dislike with the other.

They are mentally very quick and keen, and in all matters where a subtle mentality is needed they can out-distance all rivals.

They are excellent in diplomacy, and dazzle their listeners by their wit and brilliancy, but they usually leave them no wiser than they were at the start.

If taken as they are, in their own moods, they are the most delightful people imaginable, but one must not attempt to hold them or to expect them to be constant to their ideas or plans.

If you were to tell them that they said a totally different thing the day before, they would be offended and tell you, with the greatest candour, that you could not have heard aright, or were completely mistaken.

They believe they are truthful, constant, faithful, and so they may be at the moment, but every moment to them has a seperate existence.

They see quickly the weak points in those they meet, and can reduce all to nothing by wit, sarcasm, or mimicry.

They are more generous to individuals than to institutions, for they act on impulse in giving as in everything else they do.

In appearance these people generally have a rather long, narrow head and face; good, keen, sharp-looking eyes that seem to glitter when aroused by emotion or desire; there is often something bird-like in their expression; the hands as a rule, are long, thin or bony, rather like claws; restless or always doing something. In nature they are inclined to have too many "irons in the fire" at the same moment. When they are given much time to think over a project, they are often indecisive or change their minds. On account of this they are seldom reliable in their promises, or put off the execution of them until forced by circumstances to carry them out.

The higher types are clever, capable, witty, subtle, with an odd sense of humour quite their own. As a rule they are intellectual with a keen mentality that shows itself in anything they seriously take up. Worry, annoyance or undue mental strain breaks them down very rapidly, producing nervous prostration, brain exhaustion, and in some cases insanity.

They are highly strung and restless. If they are rich and can travel, they are always on the move. They love speed and rapid movement. They are good patrons for express trains, aeroplanes, and any inventions that can eliminate distance.

On Being Successful

These people seldom, themselves, know what they want to achieve. At heart they are ambitious for social position but when obtained they are already tired of it, and are ready to go in for something else or for something totally opposite.

They are always doing something, but they are restless, and as a rule want the thing they have not got.

They make clever actors, lawyers, lecturers and a certain class of public speakers, all those who play a changing role in life's drama; but if endowed with unusually strong will power, and if they can force themselves to stick to one thing, then they generally make brilliant success of whatever they undertake in any sphere of life.

They often succeed the best, as far as money is concerned, on the Stock Exchange or as Company Promoters or in the invention of new ways to get wealth in business, but their more suitable career is generally that which requires diplomacy, tact and finesse.

In all matters of affection they are human puzzles. They can love passionately and yet be inconstant at the same moment, and it is only their shield of diplomacy and exquisite tact that keeps them from often making a mess of their lives.

It is scarcely probable that they will admit this judgment of their character, unless they are in a self-analytical mood when they read this.

The lower types are unscrupulous in finance and untruthful. They often make successful gamblers and company promoters of "get-rich-quick" schemes.

They have often great "ups and downs" in life, but nothing makes much impression on them.

These people are ingenious, inventive and energetic, but they should cultivate persistency and tenacity of purpose. If such persons cultivate concentration of their mental powers, they can always succeed.

Friends and Relationships

Both types make their most lasting friendships with people born either in their own period of the year or from September 21 to October 20-27, January 21 to February 18-27, or with people born in the centre of their own triangle, from November 21 to December 20-27 (See Fig. VI, Page 112).

Either type makes hosts of friends, and are kind-hearted and generous to the person who fills their thoughts at the moment, but "out of sight, out of mind" explains their fits of "forgetfulness" as nothing else can.

They are warm hearted, sympathetic to others and intensely human. Marriage is not likely to be fovourable unless they have the good fortune to meet a person of the opposite sex who is of the same way of thinking as themselves. They are most attractive to their opposite sex and likely to have many unusual love affairs and romances and have an eventful life.

Health

People born in this part of the year are seldom physically very strong. They live on their nerves and deplete their nervous system. They are like electric batteries that must be re-charged from time to time. If they can do this by sleep, they may then escape the break down that such people are so often threatened with.

They are more inclined to suffer from what concerns the nervous system than anything else; both men and women are likely to have delicacy with the digestive organs and upper stomach. In their youth they are also inclined to catalepsy and affections of the tongue, but they generally outgrow this after they reach maturity. They are rather inclined to have trouble with the bronchial tubes and upper part of the lungs, and are subject to pneumonia, pleurisy, or illnesses brought on by an over-wrought nervous system.

Finance

June is a difficult month to describe the financial condition of people born in this part of the year because of it being the house of Mercury.

As Mercury is essentially " a planet of the mind," it all depends on what direction the mentality is stimulated. Desire may develop for purely intellectual things such as science, art, literature, music etc. In such cases ambitions will be strong and will compel the man or women to excel in any of these lines of work.

If however, the mind runs in the direction of the accumulation of material things, such as finance, the tendency will be to get into lines of work when money can be made quickly and in consequence business, and particularly speculations, will attract the individual. Such people will never be satisfied with their success, especially in the pursuit of money. They will be inclined to risk too much.

In the pursuit of intellectual side of life, the people will be inclined to exhaust their energies and so bring on some form of nervous breakdown that may impair the continuation of their efforts.

In both cases, the result in the end would amount to the same thing — the uncertainty of finance.

Colours

Their colours are silver, glistening white, and all shimmering things.

Stones

The birth stones for this period are white and red cornelians, sapphires, diamonds and all glittering jewels.

Various Concerns, Occasions, Undertakings, Activities and Interests Which Fall Under the Ruling Planets

Mercury: Travel, transport and communication of every kind: writing, television, radio, figuring, advertising, journalism, public speaking, education, and all things that concern the young.

Moon: Emotional imaginations, untidy, prosperity, success in intellectual pursuits, loss of assets, mental worries, literary, ambitious.

Some Famous Persons
Born in this Part of the year

Nargis Dutt	1
Thomas Hardy	2
George Fernandes	3
George V	3
Jefferson Davis	3
T. Kasinath	5
K. A. Abbas	7
Tom Jones	7
Gen. J.N. Chaudhuri	10
Javed Miandad	12
Dean Martin	17
Paul McCartney	18
Ralph Waldo Emerson	25
Lord Louis Mountbatten	25
Rousseau	28

JULY

The Zodiacal Sign of Cancer commences on June 21, but for seven days, being overlapped by the "cusp" of the previous sign — Gemini, it does not come into full power until on or about June 28. From this date

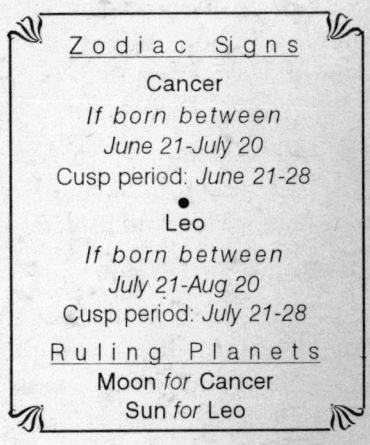

Zodiac Signs

Cancer
If born between
June 21-July 20
Cusp period: *June 21-28*

•
Leo
If born between
July 21-Aug 20
Cusp period: *July 21-28*

Ruling Planets
Moon *for* Cancer
Sun *for* Leo

onwards it is in full strength until July 20, and is then for seven days gradually losing its strength on account of becoming overlapped by the "cusp" of the incoming sign — Leo.

Personality Traits

People born in this section of the year are full of contradictions. They have deep home interests, but are at the same time restless, and have a decided longing for travel and change. They are always making homes, rarely keeping them, and usually have more than the usual trouble in their homes. They do succeed in making their domestic life.

They have, however, most sensitive nature — perhaps more so than any other class of people — and if not understood they quickly give up or get depressed. Above all, they require encouragement and appreciation.

As a rule they are "dreamers" of large plans. They evolve big ideas for the welfare of others, but if they meet opposition and criticism they suffer keenly, but silently, in themselves, and are inclined to become cynical.

Although of a deeply affectionate disposition, they are seldom demonstrative, and are wrongly considered cold and unemotional. At heart they are romantic and of a very loving and affectionate nature.

On Being Successful

They are generally over-anxious in financial matters, and make great efforts to gather in money; as a rule, they have unusual ups and downs in their early life, and it takes all their hard work to keep ahead, but once they get on their feet they generally keep there.

They are inclined to speculate, so as to make money quickly, but in all gambles they generally lose, whereas in business they are, as a rule, most successful

They are industrious and hardworking in all they undertake, but from the standpoint of chance or luck they are seldom fortunate, but the most extraordinary and unexpected changes, for good or evil, seem always ready to come into their lives.

They are generally gifted with strong imaginations, and often make excellent artists, writers, composers, or musicians.

Like the symbol of "the Crab," which this part of the Zodiac represents, they advance and retreat both in work and ideas; they may reach a certain point in some definite plan or career, and then surprise everyone by stopping, or turning back at the most critical point.

People born in this part of the year often reach very exalted positions or gain some pinnacle of fame where they cannot escape the dazzling light of publicity.

Generally, they have splendid memories and store up knowledge of all kinds in their minds. They sometimes make excellent psychics or become deeply interested in occult studies or in religion, or in some unusual philosophy of life.

Friends and Relationships

Their affections or friendships last longest with those who are born in their own period, June 21 to July 20-27, or from October 21 to November 20-27, or from February 19 to March 20-27, and also those who are in the centre of their triangle, December 21 to January 20-27. (See Fig. V, Page 111).

They have a great dislike of being dictated to, but are most devoted and faithful when treated with confidence.

They should never marry young, for their nature seems to change at different stages of life.

They have deep love for what they call "their own people," for family customs and tradition. In their home lives, however, they usually go through a great deal of trouble and are seldom surrounded by great happiness, no matter how successful they may appear in the eyes of the world.

Health

The influence of the Moon for people born in this period of the year is inclined to play a considerable role, and renders the constitution somewhat delicate. The emotional nature being stronger than the physical, most ailments are brought about by ill-controlled feelings and morbid imagination.

They are chiefly inclined towards gastric troubles, ptomaine poisoning, and diarrhoea, and they should be extremely careful in regard to shelfish and such things. Inflammatory diseases, such as rheumatism, are also likely to attack them, and they can also suffer from internal tumors, dropsy, varicose veins, and trouble with the legs and feet.

Finance

The influence of Neptune and the Moon brings about many unexpected changes in the lives of the people born in this part of the year. They should be very careful in all financial dealings including signing of papers, contracts, agreements and documents of financial dealings. They often gain from some totally unexpected sources.

They nearly always find success in investments connected with oil interests, refining of oil or coal, shipping, radium, platinum, electricity etc.

Success by investing in large public utility companies and association is generally good, but particular attention should be given to concerns which cater directly or indirectly for the needs and requirements of the masses at large.

They are painstaking and industrious in all they undertake, but are inclined to have extremes of good and bad fortune. As a rule they have great "ups and downs" in money matters, unless they have conquered the speculative tendency in their nature early in life, and accumulated wealth. If wealth does come to them it usually multiplies beyond the dreams of Midas.

Colours

The colours most in harmony for them are all shades of green, cream and white.

Stones

The birth stones most favourable for this period are pearls, diamonds, opals, crystals, cat's-eyes, and moonstones.

Various Concerns, Occasions, Undertakings, Activities and Interests Which Fall Under the Ruling Planets

Moon: Emotional imaginations, untidy, prosperity, success in intellectual pursuits, loss of assets, mental worries, literary, ambitious.

Sun: Sociable, generous, loyal, proud, luxury, comfort, clean, conquest of enemies, extravagant, wealth, fame, power.

Some Famous Persons
Born in this Part of the Year

Nathaniel Hawthorne	4
Ringo Starr	7
Pierre Cardin	7
Joseph Chamberlaen	8
Sunil Gavaskar	10
Bimal Roy	12
Gerald Ford	14
Ingrid Bergman	14
Om Shivpuri	14
Badal Sircar	15
Nelson Mandela	18
Dom Moraes	19
Edmund Hillary	20
G.B. Shaw	26
Mussolini	29
J.R.D. Tata	29
K Shankar Pillai	31

AUGUST

The Zodiacal Sign of Leo commences on July 21, but for seven days, being overlapped by the "cusp" of the previous sign — Cancer, it does not come into full power until on or about July 28. From this day onwards it is in full strength until August 20 and is then for seven days gradually losing its strength on account of becoming overlapped by the "cusp" of the incoming sign — Virgo.

Personality Traits

People born in this period represent what might be termed the heart-force of humanity. They are overflowing with sympathy, and are generally generous to a fault. They are themselves exceptionally truthful and honest, but they often get terribly deceived, and have a tendency in the end to become bitter, severe, and over-critical. They make enemies by their frankness of speech and their hatred of anything underhand or what savours of subterfuge.

As a rule they radiate warmth, affection, kindness and a strong personal magnetism which makes them very popular. Great soldiers, leaders in finance, and public men are often born in this period.

Their exaggerated faith in human nature is their stumbling block in love and friendship leading to many tragedies, heartaches and estrangements. They will defend a friend in the face of all attacks; it is only treachery, disloyalty or deceit that can ever break or crush their proud spirit.

Such persons must, however, be always actively employed. If forced by circumstances out of the heat and stress of the battle of life, they often become morbid and despondent. They also feel isolated and lonely if not actively engaged in some work.

They have the power to inspire others, and as leaders — like Napoleon, born in this Sign — they can lead their men through fire or death. They are intensely proud, and are often easily wounded at this point in their nature.

As a rule they are extremely patient and long-suffering, but if once aroused, like the lion, they know no fear and do not even know when they meet defeat or acknowledge it when they do.

They have great tenacity of purpose, determination, and will power if they once put their mind on some purpose, but they usually attempt the most daring and difficult things.

Impetuous and quick-tempered, they make enemies through their frankness and straight-forwardness.

On Being Successful

People born in this period have large ambition, their aim is to get above the common herd of humanity and in no matter how low or humble the sphere of life into which they are born, they generally rise by their will, determination and ability into high positions of authority in whatever career they adopt as their own. They are keenly attracted to other strong personalities, infact, they are ready to forgive any fault in others so long as they have individuality and purpose.

They have an extremely independent spirit, they detest control or being dictated to. They have much tenacity of purpose and will power, and if they put their mind on some plan, purpose or position, they usually reach their goal inspite of any difficulty or obstacle. They have wonderful magnetic power in inspiring others to do great deeds. They accept responsibilities and take too much on their shoulders. They blame no one but themselves for any shortcomings they may have.

Friends and Relationships

They would find their most lasting friendships with people born in their own period or from March 21 to April 19-27, with their "central affinities", January 21 to February 18-28, and November 21 to December 20-27; and, strange to say all those people born on the 1st, 10th, 19th, or 28th of any month, for the reason that these numbers accord and have a sympathetic attraction to the Number of the Sun, which is the number of this period. (See Fig. IV, Page 109).

They are exceptionally loyal to heir friends and to those whom they love. They are so magnanimous and broad-minded that they are not likely to make any serious enemies, even though they may disagree with their views. Disloyalty and deceit are the only things that can break their hearts.

They have a deep sincere, affectionate nature, a keen sense of home life and a great love of children. They are extremely sensitive both in relation to people and their surroundings.

They are generally popular with the opposite sex, with idealistic love affairs and romances bringing strong and unusual episodes in their lives.

Health

People born in this part of the year are generally endowed with good recuperation power, causing them to radiate vitality.

Their chief physical trouble is likely to proceed from irregularity of the heart-beat which tends to affect the circulation. They are inclined to suffer from pains in the head and ears, inflammation of the eyes and kidneys, trouble with the bladder, injuries to the feet and peculiar stiffness of the legs. Discordant or inharmonious surroundings will also have a detrimental effect upon their health in general.

The planetary influences governing a birth in this period of the year indicate that at times they will be inclined to suffer from acute attacks of rheumatism when the fever will run dangerously high.

They will find sun baths beneficial while plenty of fresh air will always do more goods than drugs. Grief or prolonged worry impairs their health more quickly than anything else.

Finance

People born in this period are generally financially well-placed. They get success in any legitimate business they may go in for. They are likely to gain through superiors. They quite often benefit through speculation and judicious investment. Investments connected with gold mining, brass work, diamonds, import and export and with government dealings should bring them good returns.

Their financial plans and projects should be on a large scale and favour the patronage of the general public rather than the individual.

Colours

Their most suitable colours are all shades of yellow, orange, pale green, and white.

Stones

The birth stones for this period are topazes, amber, and rubies.

Various Concerns, Occasions, Undertakings, Activities and Interests Which Fall Under the Ruling Planets

Sun: Sociable, generous, loyal, proud, luxury, comfort, clean, conquest of enemies, extravagant, wealth, fame, power.

Mercury: Travel, transport and communication of every kind: writing, television, radio, figuring, advertising, journalism, public speaking, education, and all things that concern the young.

Some Famous Persons
Born in this Part of the Year

SEPTEMBER

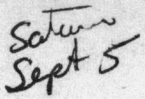

The Zodiacal Sign of Virgo commences on August 21, but for seven days, being overlapped by the "cusp" of the previous sign — Leo, it does not come into its full power until on or about August 29. From this

> **Zodiac Signs**
> **Virgo**
> *If born between*
> *Aug 21-Sept 20*
> Cusp period: *Aug 21-29*
>
> **Libra**
> *If born between*
> *Sept 21-Oct 20*
> Cusp period: *Sept 21-28*
>
> **Ruling Planets**
> Mercury *for* Virgo
> Venus *for* Libra

date onwards it is in full strength until September 20, and is then for seven days gradually losing its strength on account of becoming overlapped by the "cusp" of the incoming sign — Libra.

Personality Traits

People born in this part of the year are extremely fond of harmony in their surroundings, have excellent taste about their house and dress, and always want things in good tastes, and elegant.

They are fastidious about their personal appearance, have a great respect for rank and position, and are great supporters of the law and the law's decisions.

They are inclined to become wrapped up in themselves and their own ideas, and often become selfish in the close pursuit of their aims.

They have always "their wits about them," and are generally self-possessed and self-reliant.

They are more capable of going to extremes in good and evil than any other type. If they develop a love for money, they will stick at nothing to acquire it, and this type is often considered cunning and crafty at the expense of others.

They can adapt themselves to almost any pursuit in life. In their inner love nature they are the most difficult to understand, the very best and the very worst of men and women being in this part of the year.

In their early years nearly all are intensely virtuous and pure-minded, as might be expected, being born in the Sign of Virgo.

If they change they do so with a vengeance and become the exact reverse, but, on account of their inborn respect of the law and their natural cleverness, they succeed in covering up their lapses better than any other class. They have often a tendency to indulge in drugs or drink.

On Being Successful

People born in this period are, as a rule, generally successful in life. They have keen, good intellects, are very discriminating about those with whom they associate, and in all business matters they have good judgment, and are not easily imposed upon or deceived. They are usually materialistic in their views of life, and analyse and reason everything from their own way of thinking outwards.

They make good literary critics, being quick to see the weak points, and at the same time they are rapid readers and endowed with wonderful memories.

74

They are not so apt to be originators as they are to carry out some plan or work that appeals to them and which others have failed to finish, and in the execution of almost all things to which they put their minds they achieve success.

They make excellent lawyers and debaters, but they tend towards supporting precedents more than originating any new law.

They succeed well in business, but more from their steady, industrious persistency than from evolving new ideas.

Friends and Relationships

They will find their most lasting friendships with those born in their own Sign, also from April 20 to May 20-27, and with their "central affinities," February 19 to March 20-27 and December 21 to January 20-27 (See Fig.VII, Page 113).

Their affectionate nature is very intense but not of the emotional, demonstrative order, but once their love is awakened they are extremely loyal but inclined to be jealous. They are capable of making and holding friends. They should be careful in selection of a partner in marriage. It would be better for them to marry late in life as their ideas and views change radically after middle life.

Health

In health, as a rule, they are less liable to diseases than persons born in any other part of the year, yet the strange thing about them is that they are always imagining themselves to have every illness that they may happen to read about in the public Places.

They are very refined in their tastes as far as food is concerned, and must have things nicely put before them or they will lose their appetites.

They are extremely sensitive to their surroundings; the least inharmony or annoyance affects their nervous system and upsets their digestive organs.

They are very liable to sudden internal derangement in the intestine, and have extremes of constipation, varied by dysentery or colic.

They have a tendency to have trouble with the lungs, and to suffer from neuritis in the shoulders and arms.

As this sign of the Zodiac appears to be intimately associated with the Solar Plexus, people born in this part of the year need sunlight and fresh air more than any other class of individual.

Peace and harmony in their surroundings are most essential to the good health of people born in this period, for they seem to stand worry less than those of any other class.

They should live as much as possible in the open air, and when run down or ill, a few weeks in the country will work marvels with them.

As a rule, they retain their youth through life in the most wonderful manner.

They are true children of Nature, and the plainest food is best for their health, but they are so peculiarly refined in their tastes that even the badly served dishes will destroy their appetite.

If badly mated, or living under inharmonious marriage conditions, they easily fall into ill health or get extremely despondent. They should never drink alcohol, as it seems to be more a poison to them than to any other class.

Finance

In matters of finance this is a favourable part of the year to be born in. It gives good business ability and a careful frugal nature. It gives favourable conditions for investing in houses, lands and property. Although people born in this period are inclined to be over-anxious, there is nothing much for them to fear about financial matters. These people can fit themselves in any position and make money in almost anything. They are inclined to gain by legacies and by gifts. They are confined to any one line of work, but will more likely have many "irons in the fire".

Colours

Their most suitable colours are all very pale shades and silvery, shimmering materials.

Stones

The birth stones for this period are emeralds, diamonds, and pearls.

Various Concerns, Occasions, Undertakings, Activities and Interests Which Fall Under the Ruling Planets

Mercury: Travel, transport and communication of every kind: writing, television, radio, figuring, advertising, journalism, public speaking, education, and all things that concern the young.

Venus: Love, courtship, mating, marriage, art, music, decoration, dress, entertaining, holidays, dancing, gambling, peacemaking, pleasure of every kind, healing, social occasions of every kind, almsgiving.

Some Famous Persons
Born in this Part of the year

Rajinder Singh Bedi	1
Habib Tanvir	1
Henry George	2
S. Radhakrishnan	5
Queen Elizabeth	7
Vinoba Bhave	11
R.K. Karanjia	15
M.F. Hussain	17
Shabana Azmi	18
Yash Chopra	18
Greta Garbo	18
Sophia Loren	20
Michael Faraday	22
Ramdhari Singh Dinkar	23
Dev Anand	23
Julius Caesar	23

OCTOBER

Z o d i a c   S i g n s

Libra
If born between
Sept 21-Oct 20
Cusp period: *Sept 21-28*

•

Scorpio
If born between
Oct 21-Nov 20
Cusp period: *Oct 21-28*

R u l i n g   P l a n e t s
Venus *for* Libra
Mars *for* Scorpio

The Zodiacal Sign of Libra commences on September 21, but for seven days, being overlapped by the "cusp" of the previous sign — Virgo, it does not come into full power until on or about September 28. From this date onwards it is in full strength until October 20, and is then for seven days gradually losing power on account of becoming overlapped by the incoming sign — Scorpio.

Personality Traits

People born in this period are positive and decisive in their thoughts and actions. They have great foresight and intuition, and are generally seen at their best when acting on first impressions.

They are often very psychic, have curious presentiments, and would make very devout spiritualists, theosophists, and occultists, and yet so strongly endowed are they with the desire to reason out everything that their love of exact proof usually overwhelms their psychic powers.

They are unusually sensitive to their surroundings. If in inharmonious condition, they easily become melancholy, suffer from nervous depression and shrank into themselves. They are, as a rule, very even-tempered; they are born "peacemaker" for they detest disputes and quarrels. They are particular about their appearance and dislike seeing things in disorder. They have a many-sided nature having numerous moods. Lofty idealism and high moral principle form the fundamental basis of their character.

People born in this period generally sacrifice themselves to others through ties of affection or by their sense of duty. Because they live habitually in the present, they will care little for the ties of the past and less still for the obscurities of the future.

On Being Successful

They are often very successful as speculators, but they have little regard for the value of money, and have as a rule great ups and downs in their careers.

In symbolism they represent a "balance". They seem always trying mentally to balance things and get an even judgement.

Large numbers of them seem to drift naturally into the study of law, and in it they generally make a name as lawyers, barristers, or judges.

They are also often found in public life, but again it is with their innate desire to adjust the balance of things by making laws for the betterment of their fellows.

They have great reverence for knowledge, and often spend their lifetime in study and research in some particular subject, again weighing and balancing every side of the question in the most conscientious manner. For this reason they make excellent doctors, but generally make their name as masters of some particular line of study more than as general practitioners.

In all careers they require depth of study, thoughtfulness and balance. All professional walks of life are, as a rule, well suited to them. Their artistic side of the nature is very pronounced; they are extremely fond of music and art and often have much ability in that direction.

Friends and Relationships

They would find their most lasting friendships and unions with persons born between January 21 and February 18-27, May 21 and June 20-27, and with those born in their own Sign or with their "central affinities", March 21 to April 19-26. (See Fig. VI, Page 112).

In marriage they are seldom happy. In affection they appear to weigh and balance matters too much; they perhaps forget that the wings of love are not made for the lens of the microscope, and so they seem to court disillusion and disappointment in advance.

They crave for the peace and happiness of home life but, in doing so they generally become too exacting, and the result is, more often than not, disaster. They have the compensation, however, of making large circles of friends and acquaintances and are largely sought after as companions.

Health

People born in this period have a natural instinct for health and sanity. They manage to keep the balance and avoid serious breakdown of any kind. However, they are inclined to suffer from nerves and depression of spirits, also from pains in the back and kidneys and severe headaches. They are liable to have "Bright's disease" and peculiar maladies of the skin. Their most frequent symptoms of overstrain are connected with the kidneys, which are curiously sensitive.

They have not a great deal of physical energy, though they possess good recuperative powers. They require an exceptional amount of fresh air and should if possible, lead a simple life and be exceptionally careful in matters of diet.

The women of this sign are also inclined to suffer from affections of the internal organs and often have to submit to the severest operations.

Finance

In the question of finance, although people born in this period succeed in making money, they are seldom able to hold on to it in their advanced years. They are inclined to gain money by mental occupations and by carrying out their own individual ambitions. Their greatest danger is that no matter what money they gain, they will make no provision for the advanced year, and often die in restricted circumstances. They desire wealth to meet their needs in life, not for personal accumulation. They can gain benefits from powerful friends, from their opposite sex or from marriage. Commercial business and routine work will be distasteful for them, but they may make money and succeed from their great gifts of imagination and inspiration in the call of emergency. They should, however, avoid, all forms of speculation or gambles of every kind. They are inclinied to occupy positions of responsibility and authority, but never for very long, unless they develop control over their impetuous nature, quick temper and lack of diplomacy.

Colours

The most suitable colours for them are all shades of blue, violet, purple and mauve.

Stones

The birth stones for this period are the opal and the pearl.

Various Concerns, Occasions, Undertakings, Activities and Interests Which Fall Under the Ruling Planets

Venus: Love, courtship, mating, marriage, art, music, decoration, dress, entertaining, holidays, dancing, gambling, peacemaking, pleasure of every kind, healing, social occasions of every kind, almsgiving.

Mars: Sports, games, hunting, fighting, wrestling, all that requires force, and strong and prompt action: mechanical work, "stunting", surgery, public agitations and movements.

Some Famous Persons
Born in this Part of the Year

Shivaji Ganesan	1
Annie Besant	1
Mahatma Gandhi	2
Graham Greene	2
Lal Bahadur Shastri	2
Begum Akhtar	7
Raj Kumar	8
John Lennon	9
Amjad Ali Khan	9
R.K. Narayan	10
Amitabh Bachchan	11
Jayaprakash Narayan	11
Vijay Merchant	12
Ashok Kumar	13
Margret Thatcher	13
General Eisenhower	14
J. Kenneth Galbraith	15
Oscar Wilde	16
Ebrahim Alkazi	18
Premjit Lal	20
Samuel Taylor Coleridge	21
Martin Luther	22
Faraday	22
Picasso	25
Shah of Iran	26
President Roosevelt	27
Capt. James Cook	28
Truman Capote	30
Chiang Kai-Shek	31

NOVEMBER

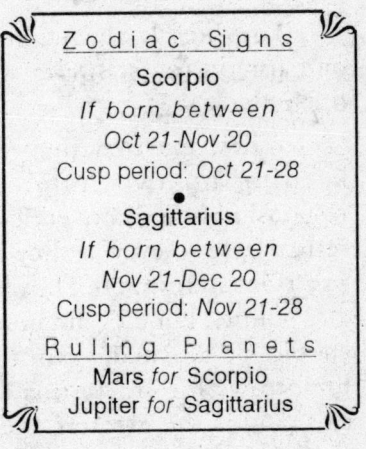

The Zodiacal Sign of Scorpio commences on October 21, but for seven days, being overlapped by the "cusp" of the previous sign — Libra, it does not come into its full power until on or about October 28. From this date onwards it is in full strength until November 20 and is then for seven days gradually losing its strength on account of becoming overlapped by the "cusp" of the incoming sign — Sagittarius.

Personality Traits

People born in this section of the year seem to be a mass of contradictions. The best and the worst seem to make this period their chosen battlefield.

Upto nearly twenty years of age they are usually extremely pure-minded, virtuous, and religious, but once their nature is roused they are often found to swing in the opposite direction.

Their worst fault is that they are too adaptable to the people with whom they come in contact. If they are thrown with evil-minded people, for the time being, they adapt themselves too much of their companions, but as a rule they right themselves when nearly capsized, and generally get out of the most difficult situations at the last moment.

They nearly always, however, lead double lives — one for the eyes of the world and the another for themselves.

When married they lean often to the idea of keeping up two homes, one with the greater responsibility and conventionality, the other a Bohemian retreat, where even if they live alone, they are at least free from all restraint. They have clever ideas in business and politics, but they are best as advisers of others. They should be warned against "putting off things until tomorrow" for procrastination is one of their besetting sins, and is the greatest enemy of people born in this period.

They are inclined to be selfish but, in contradiction to this, if they succeed they are more generous in paying back tenfold for any help they may have received.

On Being Successful

They have great magnetic power, and as speakers appeal to the emotions and sentiments of their public more than to logic, but they sway their audiences as they choose.

They have excellent power in writing, are intensely dramatic in their gifts of description, and are unusually versatile in their talents.

In dangers and in sudden crises they are cool and very determined, and many of the very best surgeons have been found in this period.

They are often great humanitarians, with great plans for making the world right, and praise will often force them on to do great things in the world for their fellow-man.

They are mental fighters, and are most subtle in arguments. They make good organisers and generals on paper, but detest bloodshed and strife in actual life.

For this reason they gain a reputation as peacemakers, and, infact, they usually excel in settling other people's quarrels and bringing enemies together to shake hands.

People of this Sign should, above all, be encouraged to have ambition, for it is the one thing that will save them: for if they will make any sacrifice or deny themselves any pleasure, and so accomplish more work than any other class.

They usually place too great a value on the opinion of the world, and for this fault they become the easy prey of blackmailers.

Sooner or later, they generally become interested in occult matters, they readily develop unusual clairvoyant powers, and quite often gain fame and distinction as writers, painters or poets. They are natural philosophers, deep students of Nature, and observe and analyse other persons' character better than any other class.

Persons born in this sign generally have, or make, two sources of income. As a rule they go through a great deal of trouble, difficulty and often privation in their early years. Such trials seem to increase their will-power and ambition, and sooner or later success and fame nearly always crown their efforts.

Friends and Relationships

They will find their most lasting friendships and unions with people born in their own period and between June 21 and July 20-27, from February 19 to March 20-27, and with the centre of their "Life's Triangle", namely: those born from April 20 to May 20-27. (See Fig. V, Page 111).

No class of people make more friends or have more enemies than those born in this period, but their strong personality carries them through like a resistless wave.

With their words, letters, or writings they can wound like the sting of a serpent, but on the slightest show of emotion or feeling all is forgotten, and they are kindness itself.

The sex quality is an enormous factor in their lives. The women attract the men and the men attract the women; but in cases where the will and ambition are dominant these people can keep the curb on their strong sex-natures, and reap success accordingly.

The sex-nature of these people must, however, be kept well under control; otherwise there are no excesses to which in the end they may not give way.

In their home life the men are inclined to be dogmatic and expect to rule, but their influence over women is so great, that they are almost always forgiven, and the most injured wife of such a man would fight for him to the last.

With their strong magnetic influence they possess generally a strange psychological power over others; they make natural healers, for they give of their great vitality to others, and when their emotions or sympathies are roused they love to give and help, and will face any danger to be of assistance.

They are generally loved and adored by those who love them, but there are few born under this sign who at some stage in their career escape being attacked by some insidious form of calumny or scandal.

Health

In their early years, people born in this period are usually delicate and thin, but put on weight after reaching middle age.

Both men and women have danger of suffering from the sex organs and with kidneys. They are liable to suffer from such things as fistula, hemorrhoids, inflammation of the bladder, and trouble with the glands of the body. Their illnesses are generally related to the large intenstine and excretory part of the system. The upper part of the lungs is usually a weak spot, as is also the bronchial tubes. Later the heart is inclined to be their weakest organ, and they should be careful not to overstrain it in exercise, or in work. In all cases persons born in Scorpio, after their twenty-first year, exhibit an extraordinary resistance to disease.

Finance

People born in this period of the year, as a rule experience the most unusual "ups and downs" of fortune. They are inclined to be too trustful and over-hopeful. They are easily persuaded into schemes that have no solid foundation. They are also over-generous and inclined to be too lavish in their expenditure. They make money by their mental abilities but they seldom can hoard it up to any great extent. It entirely depends upon them whether they will be a great success or a failure. There is no middle path for them - it will be one extreme or the other. They are likely to win their way by their dogged persistence.

Women born in this period very often marry well, especially if they marry late in life.

Colours

The colours most suitable for persons are all shades of crimson and blue.

Stones

The birth stones for this period are the turquoise, the ruby, and all red stones.

Various Concerns, Occasions, Undertakings, Activities and Interests Which Fall Under the Ruling Planets

Mars: Sports, games, hunting, fighting, wrestling, all that requires force, and strong and prompt action: mechanical work, "stunting", surgery, public agitations and movements.

Jupiter: Business and trading of every kind, investments, ceremonies and functions, seeking favour, settlements in litigation, ceremonial and philanthropic occasions of every kind where it is desired to help others and incidentally help one's self.

Some Famous Persons
Born in this Part of the Year

DECEMBER

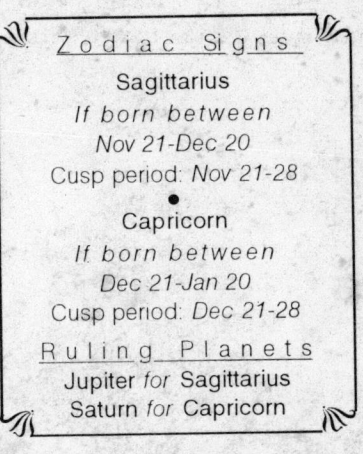

The Zodiacal Sign of Sagittarius commences on November 21, but for seven days, being overlapped by the "cusp" of the previous sign — Scorpio, it does not come into its full power until on or about November 28. From this date onwards it is in full power until December 20, and is then for seven days gradually losing its strength on account of being overlapped by the incoming Sign — Capricorn.

Personality Traits

Those born in this section of the year are executive, fearless, and determined in all they undertake.

They are apt to be too decisive and too outspoken in their speech, and so are often misjudged in their criticism, and make bitter enemies.

They are generally very honourable, but chiefly when they feel others are placing implicit confidence in them. Brutally truthful, they resent deception, and unmask any attempt to deceive others even when such action is against their own interests. There are two distinct classes that exist in this period. The people of one section have their ideals of life extremely high, and any appeal to do good is met with an immediate response; but they are more inclined to be generous toward private charities than to do good privately, for they are mostly suspicious of individuals and so dread being deceived by a plausible story that they prefer to send the beggar with their card to the secretary of some institution to which they subscribe, than to take responsibility on their own shoulders.

Those of this first class are, however, the salt of the earth in their care for their employees and people under them.

The people of the second class born in this period are easily recognised; first, by their sharp criticism of every one else's efforts for good and by their petty meanness in all matters that concern money. If you ask them for a five pound note for a charity for which their name will be mentioned in public, or a shilling for a beggar, the second class will always give the five-pound note even if they should see the beggar starving before their eyes.

They are great church-goers, even from the standpoint that their example may be beneficial to the world around them.

They venerate law and order, make the best of mothers, and train their children on the strictest lines of obedience, punctuality and upright living.

On Being Successful

They concentrate all their attention on whatever they are doing at the moment, and seem to see no other way but theirs until their effort is made.

Their minds are so intensely quick that they will often be found breaking in on the conversation of others with what they think is the end of the story or the solution of the question.

They are, however, the great workers of the earth; they never seem to tire until they wear themselves out, or drop with fatigue.

They have great enterprise in business, but never feel themselves confined to any one line. For this reason one often finds the men of this period change from clergymen to stockbrokers, or from professors to followers of trade; while the women successful in one line of work will just as quickly throw themselves heart and soul into some entirely new study.

As a rule, perhaps from their intense concentration and will power, they are successful in whatever they do, and they should always be allowed a free hand in choosing their vocation.

People of this second class are eaten up with selfish ambition. In any country in which they live they force their way into government positions. They toady to titles, and are snobs beyound description. They are also hypocrites and religious bigots of the worst class, but the simplest student of humanity after a little observation, will never confound them with those of the other class in the same Sign.

Nearly all classes in this Sign are devoted to music, even if it is only in appreciation. They often make extremely brilliant musicians, and even when this art has not been developed they will still be largely found as makers of musical instruments or as the greatest patrons of music. They will pay for church organs, boxes at the opera, and charity concerts with as much zest as children buy bonbons.

They are, however, inclined to go to extremes in all things, and make sudden decisions, or change their minds rapidly, for which they may have regrets, but they are too proud to acknowledge their error.

People born in this period, even when successful, should never cease to be actively employed–inactivity for them would mean despondency and an early decay.

Friends and Relationships

Their most lasting unions and friendships would be made with people born from March 21 to April 19-26, and July 21 to August 20-27, or in their own period, and they will also find excellent companions in those born in the centre of their triangle–namely, from May 21 to June 20-27. (See Fig. IV, Page 109).

People born in this part of the year generally enjoy great popularity; they often become "Public idols" and have fame and position thrust upon them. They are inclined to be decisive and outspoken in their words and in consequence often make bitter and unforgiving enemies.

The men of this Sign nearly always marry on impulse and regret it ever afterwards, but they are too proud to show their regrets and too conventional to appeal to the courts of assistance so they often pass for models of married happiness even when they are the most wretched.

The women of this Sign are, as a rule, the nobler of the two sexes; they do all they can to make their husbands or their children successful and are willing to sacrifice themselves to that end. They are generally chaste and pure in their marriage vows and have an intense love of home and even when unhappily married they try to make the best of a bad bargain.

Health

The influence of Jupiter on the lives of people born in this period of the year, promises that the only dangers which threaten their health arise from over-activity of mind and body. They are also rather careless in the matter of exposure to cold and heat and thus likely to suffer from acute bronchitis. They will be also inclined to suffer from rheumatism, skin troubles, delicacy of the throat and lungs. In their latter years, they may suffer from nervous system, sciatica and paralysis. They could escape from such things by a study of temperance in their mode of living. They should keep the blood pure, avoid drugs and live hygienically. They also need to give their mind more rest and practise the art of relaxation as much as possible.

Finance

People born in this period of the Zodiac have the greatest chance of making money from the work of their brains. They have much originality of ideas and should follow their own intentions in everything they do. They seldom do so well with partners and associates, but are much loved by employees, servants and those under their authority.

They often gain through legacies and gifts but as a general rule they do not accumulate much wealth.

If they do so, it is usually depleted in their advanced years.

Colours

Their most suitable colours are all shades of violet and mauve and violet-purple.

Stones

Their most favourable stones are amethysts and sapphires.

Various Concerns, Occasions, Undertakings, Activities and Interests Which Fall Under the Ruling Planets

Jupiter: Business and trading of every kind, investments, ceremonies and functions, seeking favour, settlements in litigation, ceremonial and philanthropic occasions of every kind where it is desired to help others and incidentally help one's self.

Saturn: Deep study, concentration, exact and just reasoning, mining, dealing in property and real estate, farming and gardening, drawing, mathematics, occasions requiring an absolutely balanced and unemotional state of mind.

Some Famous Persons
Born in this Part of the Year

Thomas Carlyle	4
Sheikh Abdullah	5
Henery VI	6
Sir Walter Scott	6
Warren Hastings	6
Joseph Conrad	6
Max Mueller	6
Uday Shankar	8
Vijay Amritraj	10
C. Rajagopalachari	10
Dilip Kumar	11
Mulka Raj Anand	12
Frank Sinatra	12
John Osborn	12
Raj Kapoor	14
Beethoven	16
Nissim Ezekiel	16
Humphry Davy	17
Joseph Stalin	21
Mohammad Rafi	24
Sir Issac Newton	25
Henry Miller	26
Louis Pasteur	28
Vizzy Vijaynagaram	28
King Birendra of Nepal	28
President Wilson	28
Gladstone	29
Rudyard Kipling	30

Important To Readers

It has been established by scientific observation that there are only Nine Planets in our Earth's Solar System that relate to life in this world. It has also been demonstrated by scientists that an exactly similar Solar System is repeated in the molecules revolving round all atoms in nature.

In the same way there are only Nine Numbers by which all calculations on this earth are made. Beyond the numbers of 1 to 9 the rest are repetitions, a 10 being simply a 1 (1+0=1) an 11 is 1 plus 1, a 2; a 12 is 1 plus 2, a 3, and so on. Every number no matter how large, can be reduced to a single figure by what is called "natural addition" adding from left to right. The final single digit that remains is called the 'spirit or soul number' of the previous numbers added together.

It therefore follows that all Birthdates come into the 1-9 scale and respond to the numbers given to the Nine Planets of our Solar System. The number of a person born on 28th will be (2+8=10 and again 1+0=1) one. Similarly the number of a person born on 17 will be (1+7=8) eight. A person born on the 10th, 19th or 28th of a month is as equally a "Number One" individual, as if they had been born on the single 1.

Relationships Based on Occult Significance of Numbers and Birth Dates

At first sight it may seem extravagant to say that people may easily and quickly learn whether or not they will be in sympathetic harmony with those they meet by applying the following few simple rules which I have found, by long experience, cover one of the mysterious sides of occultism in regard to Numbers.

Even a few tests will prove to those who care to try that there is a great deal in the curious theory which I am about to lay before the readers of this book.

When dealing with such subjects I endeavour to write in such a clear and simple way that even those who have had no experience whatever in occult studies may be able to understand and act on my remarks, and make experiments for themselves.

Only Nine Numbers

In our solar system, there are only nine planets and it is necessary to grasp the idea that there are really only nine Numbers, by which all our calculations are made. They are the foundation numbers of all sciences, and all calculations lie between the Number 1 and the number 9. All others are only a repetition of these numbers. For example, a number 10 is a 1 with 0 added, and 11 is when added together a 2; a 12 is a 3; a 13 is a 4; and so on up to any number that one may examine.

We may illustrate this as given below:

1   10 (1+0=1), 19 (1+9=10, 1+0=1), 28 (2+8=10, 1+0=1) ...

2   11 (1+1=2), 20 (2+0=2), 29 (2+9=11, 1+1=2) ...

3   12 (1+2=3), 21 (2+1=3), 30 (3+0=3) ...

4   13 (1+3=4), 22 (2+2=4), 31 (3+1=4) ...

5   14 (1+4=5), 23 (2+3=5), 32 (3+2=5) ...

6   15 (1+5=6), 24 (2+4=6), 33 (3+3=6) ...

7   16 (1+6=7), 25 (2+5=7), 34 (3+4=7) ...

8   17 (1+7=8), 26 (2+6=8), 35 (3+5=8) ...

9   18 (1+8=9), 27 (2+7=9), 36 (3+6=9) ...

The occult meaning of each of these nine numbers, as they occur in the Birth dates of men and women, determine the secrets of human nature.

These numbers were given to the nine planets that control our solar system. The day of birth as key number is related to the planet bearing the same number.

Relationship between Numbers and Planets

1. The number 1 stands in symbolism for the *Sun*.

2. The number 2 stands in symbolism for the *Moon*

3. The number 3 stands in symbolism for the Planet *Jupiter*.

4. The number 4 stands in symbolism for the planet *Uranus*. It is considered related to the *Sun*.

5. The number 5 stands in symbolism for the planet *Mercury*.

6. The number 6 stands in symbolism for the planet *Venus*.

7. The number 7 stands in symbolism for the planet *Neptune*. The Planet Neptune has been considered as associated with the *Moon*.

8. The number 8 stands in symbolism for the planet *Saturn*.

9. The number 9 stands in symbolism for the planet *Mars*.

Birth Dates

Taking the above-explanation as a starting basis, the reader may now be able to follow my theory—a theory, by the way, that has taken me years to work out and prove, which is that independent of what part of the year one may be born in, a curious sympathy and attraction will be found to exist between all those who have the same number for their birth date. For example a person born, say, on the Ist of any month will find others that are born on the Ist, 10th (1+0=1), 19th (1+9=10; 1+0=1), or 28th (2+8=10, 1+0=1) of any month more sympathetic than people not born on these dates.

The next rule is that the double numbers 1 and 4 of the Sun and of the Moon numbers 2 and 7 are sympathetic to one another, as they are also to their own series, when taken as single numbers. For example, a person born on the 2nd is sympathetic to those born on the 7th, 11th (1+1=2), 16th (1+6=7), 20th (2+0=2), 25th (2+5=7), and 29th (2+9=11, 1+1=2)), which make all twos and sevens.

These persons would be sympathetic also to people born under what is called the sun's numbers 1 and 4, namely Ist, 4th, 10th (1+0=1), 13th (1+3=4), 19th (1+9=10, 1+0=1), 22nd (2+2=4), 28th (2+8=10, 1+0=1) and 31st (3+1=4) which make ones and fours.

People born under the Sun's numbers 1 and 4 and the Moon's numbers 2 and 7 are always attracted and "natural friends" to one another but all other numbers attract their own class.

Affinities in Human Beings

Such attraction is, however, more mental than physcial. It is, as it were, that the planets of the same numbers rule the mind and make those born on the same dates have a similarity and sympathy of thought to one another.

Physical attraction takes place if the birth date of two people should be in certain months of the year, and if in such a case the numbers should also be found to be in sympathy then we would have both mental and physical attraction, which would make a union of friendship unbreakable. This is an illustration of that often misused expression that "marriages are made in heaven."

Such marriages are, in fact, made in the heavens by the planet and places of the year creating affinities in human beings, which has been so eloquently expressed in the following well-known verse:

"Two shall be born the whole wide world apart
And speak in different tongues, and take no thought
Each of the other's being, and no heed.
And these o'er unknown seas to unknown lands
Shall cross, escaping wreck, defying death,
And all unconsciously shape every act,
And bend each wandering step unto this end
That one day out of darkness they shall meet
And read life's meaning in each other's eyes."

In the following chapter I shall deal with this curiously interesting subject, and also show the affinities of those born in certain months with others.

RELATIONSHIPS BASED ON LIFE'S TRIANGLES AND AFFINITIES

The reader knows by now the path along which the sun moves is called the ecliptic. In reality, it is the pathway of the earth around the sun. The reader has also learnt that the broad belt extending to about $9°$ on either side of the ecliptic is known as the Zodiac. For astrological purposes the Zodiac is divided into 12 equal parts called Signs. These Signs are divided into four groups, representing the four basic elements — Fire, Water, Air and Earth. In turn each of the elements rules three signs:

Fire   –   Aries, Leo, Sagittarius

Water   –   Cancer, Scorpio, Pisces

Air   –   Libra, Aquarius, Gemini

Earth   –   Capricorn, Taurus, Virgo

These four basic elements are represented by four triangles — Triangle of Fire, Triangle of Water, Triangle of Air and Triangle of Earth.

These triangles fit together and represent the most perfect symbolism of the four elements necessary to human life — Fire, Water, Air and Earth.

In order to fix these four triangles clearly in one's mind, I would advise my readers to first draw an equilateral triangle (a triangle with all sides and angles equal) and place at its three corners or vertices the

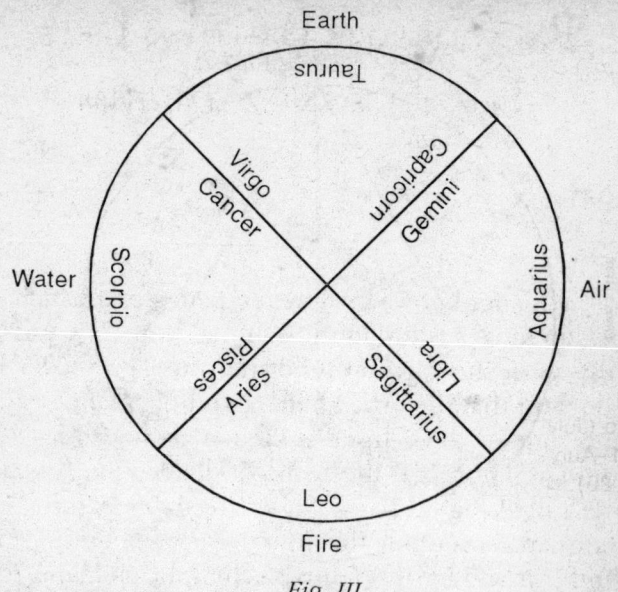

Fig. III
The Life's Triangles

sections of the year representing the three Zodiac Signs. Thus there will be four triangles representing the four elements (Fire, Water, Air and Earth) which in turn will rule the twelve Zodiac Signs.

Triangle of Fire

Taking the Triangle of Fire, place Aries (March 21 to April 19) at the top vertex, Leo (July 21 to Aug 20) at the left vertex and Sagittarius (Nov 21 to Dec 20) at the right vertex of the triangle. You will then have what are called the "Fire Affinities" in their proper places. By affinity I mean a natural or spontaneous attraction and sympathy between persons born under these Zodiac Signs. Such attractions, however, are more mental than physcial.

108

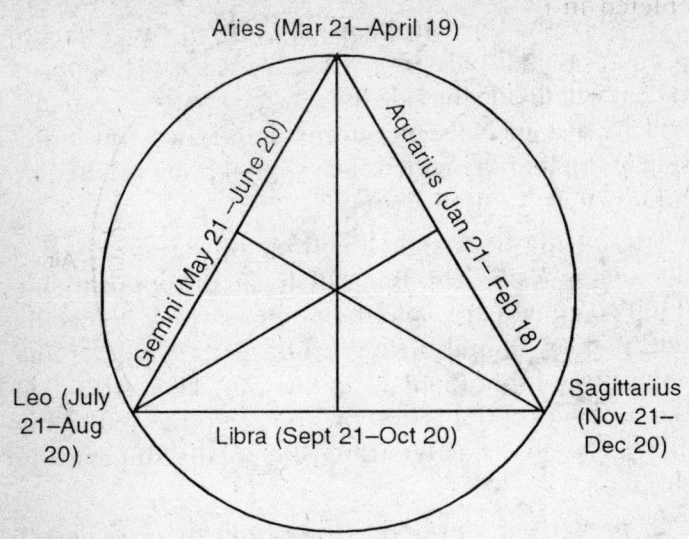

Fig. IV.
The Fire Triplicity

EXPLANATION

First House   : March 21 to April 19 and "cusp" to April 26.

Second House : July 21 to August 20 and "cusp" to August 27.

Third House   : November 21 to December 20 and "cusp" to December 27.

CENTRAL AFFINITIES

Of First House   : September 21 to October 20 and "cusp" to October 27.

Of Second House : January 21 to February 19 and "cusp" to February 26.

Of Third House   : May 21 to June 20 and "cusp" to June 27.

Since the lines of the triangle are of equal length, if you draw a line from any one vertex to its opposite side, it will divide the side in two equal parts. The centre will be at equal distance from the vertices on either side of the line so divided. The central point on the line is known as "Central Affinity".

Now draw a straight line from top vertex, Aries, to the side opposite. This line will divide the opposite side into two equal parts, and the point at which it cuts the side is the "Central affinity". On this central affinity point place Libra (Sept 21 to Oct 20). Thus Aries and Libra are in central affinity with each other indicating that these are equally strong but totally opposite in character.

Similarly if you draw a line from the Leo vertex which divides the opposite side into two equal halves, the point where it cuts is central affinity. On this place Aquarius (Jan 21 to Feb 18) which would indicate Leo and Aquarius in central affinity with each other–equally strong but opposite in character. If you look at the illustration you will see points of central affinity in the Fire Triplicity. Similar will be the case with Sagittarius and Gemini which are in central affinity with each other.

Triangle of Water

The symbolic triangle representing the element of water is formed in the following manner. Place Cancer (June 21 to July 20) at the top vertex, Scorpio (Oct 21 to Nov 20) at the left vertex and Pisces (Feb 19 to March 20) at the right. They are called "Water Affinities" in their proper places. You again draw a line from each vertex to the opposite sides, as indicated in the illustration and thus formed are their "Central Affinities".

Not True Affinities

All these cases cited may, as I say, get on together, and even be helpful to one another; but still these are not what one can call true affinities, and, such being the case, they are always liable to seperate, whereas those born in the same triangles, and especially when having the sympathetic numbers, when once they come together can never part, or if they do (under some unusual stress of circumstances) they generally come together again in spite of every influence that may try to keep them asunder.

People under the symbolism of Fire and Water will, however, never blend, and if forced to live together by necessity or marriage they will just as certainly seperate, and are likely in the end to become enemies.

Conclusion

It naturally follows that if a person should make a special study of any one subject, from long experience, cultivation and studious research, he will in the end unravel, at least to some extent, the so-called mysteries of the subject on which he has so concentrated his attention.

To a student of Art, Art reveals her mysteries of colour, form, design, pose, and a thousand and one subtleties that escape the ordinary observer. To a student of Biology every leaf tells its own story, every tree its age, every flower its own pedigree.

To a student of Science, what is magic to the uninitiated becomes a natural phenomenon with general laws, governed by rules or calculations that all who choose can learn and understand.

In presenting this book to the public I need then offer no other apology for so doing, than that of having been a student of this particular branch of thought for a very long period, and having proved so-called theories by countless experiments and experiences, I feel I am at last in a position to give to the world at large the result of such studies.

It is admitted by all that the occult side of things has been the one side of life the least explored or investigated. That there is an occult or hidden part in actual relation to human life is on every side a conceded fact, but before this mystery — the greatest of all — the majority of thinkers have held themselves aloof.

In our age the physical and mechanical sciences have called for the greatest attention, yet such things as wireless communication and radium, today household words, have been stumbled across by so-called chance.

Already wireless communication has saved hundreds of lives, radium has done likewise, the mysteries of yesterday have become the commonplaces of today, and so knowledge in the eternal fitness of things becomes the servant of those who serve.

In pursuit of the laws which have controlled thought in recent centuries, man has, in earning his success on the physical and mechanical plane, forgotten the loss he has sustained from the lack of study and observation on the occult or psychic side of humanity. He is more occupied today in building implements for the destruction of life than he is in the problems of life itself, or in the finding out of those laws which create, control, and sustain life.

When Newton discovered gravitation, it was not supposed for a moment that he had solved the problem of the spheres, and it is sometimes forgotten that when he came to realise that beyond our system of stars, sun, moon and planets there were again the "fixed stars" with their countless systems, in the magnitude of the problem, he could only decide that there was again some occult law behind all, greater than any known law that could even be imagined.

I trust my readers who have followed my theories through this book have grasped the fundamental fact underlying these pages, that the knowledge I have endeavoured to give to the public is of *a practical nature* with the decided object of helping my fellow men to make the best of themselves and render their lives as successful as possible.

Up to now occultism has been associated with the idea that its students must belong to the domain of dreamers of dreams, or those who live in some world of their own. In consequence of this idea the average "man in the street" has put aside such studies as not being useful, practical, or belonging to the money-making side of life.

It has also been drummed into his ears that all such studies bordered on witchcraft and were in some way or the other associated with the Devil.

Being brought up to go to church every Sunday and hearing every time he went that he was "a miserable sinner", doomed to punishment and torment both in this life and the worked to come, he in the end believed that he was "a miserable sinner", and so dared not seek for any knowledge that might enable him to shake off the chains of conventionality and customs that ground him down and kept him in mental and intellectual slavery.

He had perhaps no means of knowing that some of the greatest kings of the world owed their success and wealth to advice given by their Astrologers, or that the Egyptian Magicians had greater power than either priest or potentate. He had perhaps never read that the great Queen Elizabeth consulted her astrologer and palmist, Dr. John Dee, on all important matters of State, and that the destiny of England had been guided from time to time by those students of occultism whom he had been taught to believe were but fit companions for black cats, and were workers of the Devil.

He had perhaps never read of that great English astrologer, William Lilly, who had, predicted the Fire of London *fifteen years before it took place,* or that the House of Commons had called him before that great assembly believing that, as he had predicted the calamity with such accuracy, he could explain to them what had caused such a catastrophe.

Further, his English History had never told him that Charles-I had given the first thousand pounds his government sent him to Hampton Court to the same Lilly, the astrologer, asking him to predict his fate, and that had the King taken the warnings given to him by Astrology he might never have lost his head and descended to posterity as Charles the Martyr.

Again, it is probable he never knew that Queen Anne maintained an astrologer upon the roll of the Privy Purse, and that she had such faith in the celebrated Von Galgebrok that she asked him to predict the year of her death. This he did with perfect accuracy three years before the event, which took place on the 1st August, 1714.

Life is but the child of Mystery—we know not its origin — we know not its end. We see "as in a glass darkly" the threads of Destiny weaving the known and the unknown — and we wonder why.

We feel there is Design in all things — but it is only in looking back on the past that the wonders of "the pattern" become manifest.

We are indeed "of little faith", we children of men. We forget that we were made "in the image and likeness of God", and, in the forgetting, we have sold our birthright for "the mess of pottage" of man-made beliefs.

We do not dare to think of ourselves, for our "teachers" alone have wisdom? But alas! they locked the doors of knowledge, and the keys have rusted for want of use.

Behind all the Gods of patience—the God of Eternity—waits.

Slowly the ages pass: "A thousand years are but a day". Nations rise and fall. Teachers come and go. Time weaves Destiny into Design until in the end Perfection shines through the wrap and weft and *the God-thought underlying all becomes manifest.*

If, then one of the so-called "occult studies", such as I have tried to explain, has helped, in no matter how small a degree, to call attention to those hidden laws of life that illustrate the Divine Design, then when "the Call" come—I will go my way, content that the years of study I have given to this work were not wasted and were not in vain.

I have seen so many wrecked and broken lives, where, had the people possessed even a slight knowledge of their own dispositions, they might have been saved, that I have felt it a duty to publish in a cheap and simple form the indications of character and tendencies which may be easily learned by a study of these "periods of birth", as set forth in the following pages.

I believe that any aid that may help towards the observation of character is *not only useful but even essential if one wishes to keep abreast and succeed in this age of ever-increasing competition.*

Those people who have some means at their command to learn their own characters and the dispositions of others must certainly be thrice armed in the battle of life, and consequently more successful than the people who know nothing of such things. Therefore, I have no hesitation in saying that with this book in one's possession, one has a means towards winning success and also happiness.

With even a slight knowledge of what I designate in these pages as Life's Natural Affinities, the road to the divorce courts would not be so crowded as it is at present, parents would more easily understand their children and children their parents, and a great deal of suffering and friction might be avoided.

In conclusion, I trust I am not presuming too much when I venture to hope that this unpretentious volume may be the means of helping a large proportion of my fellow-beings to realise that in the study of the mysteries of life we are giving praise and glory to the Creator of Life, who in his infinite wisdom created all things to be used by man for the highest development of his kind.

□ □ □

CHEIRO

Count Louis Hamon, better known as "Cheiro", is regarded as the most successful palmist, numerologist and astrologer of 21st century. He was one of the first to translate and interpret in English the Hindu works of palmistry. He was initiated into this vast and mystique world of Astrology and Numerology when he came to India and stayed with Joshi family in Bombay. He studied Indian ancient treatise of palmistry "The Samudrika Shastra". In fact Cheiro came to India with the sole purpose of studying Hindu palmistry and philosophy. Thereafter starting his practice and continuing his study and research, he wrote many remarkable books on numerology, astrology and palmistry. During the course of his long career as a professional palmist, he had the privilege of meeting innumerable celebrities including kings, queens, ministers, artists and many famous and infamous persons.

Cheiro's book on numbers is a masterpiece on the science of numerology, explaining the occult significance of numbers and their influence and relation to human life. The system of numerology as explained by Cheiro is easy to follow and needs no intricate mathematical calculations. In his other book "You and Your Star", Cheiro explains Zodiacal Astrology in a lucid style which is understandable to all readers.

The Book of the Zodiac
Cheiro's You and Your Star

Rs. 55.00

In this book, "I have set out, not only the basic meaning of each month as handed down to mankind by the observations of astrologers from far distant ages to the present day, but also the meaning ascribed to each day of the year from the influence of the planets according to Chaldean Numerology".

'As far as I know, this is the first time that these combinations have ever been given to the world in an attempt to make what may be called Zodiacal Astrology of assistance to the vast mass of humanity who have not the time or the inclination to go into mathematical calculations that would be necessary in working out any other astrological system'.

— *Cheiro*
From the Foreword of the book.

Complete and unabridged authorised edition of Count Louis Hamon's, better known as 'Cheiro', classic work on astrology.

Kabala
Ancient Secrets of Numerology

Sepharial   Rs. 45.00

Kabala is an ancient work of Jewish mysticism and occult lore. Unlike other ancient systems of numerology which limit their study to the influence of numbers 0-to-9, the Jewish or the Hebrew Kabala extends the significance and interpretation of numbers to twenty-two, linking these with the twenty-two letters of the Hebrew alphabet.

In this book Sepharial explains how the knowledge of numbers, their sympathies and antipathies, discord and harmonies, can be applied in a variety of ways in our daily affairs with rewarding and profitable results.

"...explains how one can profit on speculative activities and turn the financial wheel of fortune in his favour by finding out his lucky and money numbers based on the day of the week and the hour in which one is born".

— The Hindu

Astrology For You

Shakuntala Devi   **Rs. 50.00**

Astrology is not a complex science as it often made out to be, and, in the hands of the world-famous 'human computer' – Shakuntala Devi, it becomes even simpler and easier to understand and practise it. This book discusses zodiacs, planets, asterisms, the rising signs, Bhavas, Yogas, Dasas and their effects and transits. It would help the reader not only to cast a horoscope, but also to read one. There are tables of correction for various cities and for sidereal time, Nakshatra divisions and Vimshottari Dasa, Navamsas etc. It is a complete book that leaves nothing to become an amateur astrologer.

Shakuntala Devi, though well-known as a mathematical genius the world over, is also an astrologer, now practising in Bombay and Delhi. She learnt this science in the lap of her grandfather when quite young; hers is a well-known family of priests and astrologers in South India. This is her first book on the subject aimed at the layreader and presented in a style that is easy to follow.

"The author has given methodologies of making horoscope and reading into it in very simplified terms".

— Patriot

Indian Predictive Astrology

Prof. Vishnu Sharma   Rs. 50.00

Predictive Astrology is not an art of fortune-telling. Contrary to the popular belief, it is an organised and a systematic body of knowledge with its own time-tested principles and well-developed rules.

Based on the influence of the Ascendant, the *Janma Nakshatras,* and other planetary combinations, Predictive Astrology identifies the inherent capabilities of an individual and provides the freedom to select a course of action best suited to one's strength.

In simple language, the book explains how to choose favourable options in education, career, profession and business; to predict wealth and prosperity, success in love, romance and marriage, the state of health and longevity, and happiness and harmony in life. It provides guidelines to convert opportunities to advantage. It thus enables us to be a master, rather than be a prisoner of our destiny — and therein lies the critical importance of Indian Predictive Astrology and of this book.

Dear Reader,

Welcome to the world of **Orient Paperbacks** — India's largest selling paperbacks in English. We hope you have enjoyed reading this book and would want to know more about **Orient Paperbacks.**

There are more than 400 **Orient Paperbacks** on a variety of subjects to entertain and inform you. The list of authors published in **Orient Paperbacks** includes, amongst others, distinguished and well-known names as Dr. S. Radhakrishnan, R.K. Narayan, Raja Rao, Manohar Malgonkar, Khushwant Singh, Anita Desai, Kamala Das, Dr. O.P. Jaggi, Norman Vincent Peale, Sasthi Brata and Dr. Promila Kapur. **Orient Paperbacks** truly represent the best of Indian writing in English today.

We would be happy to keep you continuously informed of the new titles and programmes of **Orient Paperbacks** through our monthly newsletter, **Orient Literary Review.** Send in your name and full address to us today. We will start sending you **Orient Literary Review** completely free of cost.

Available at all bookshops or by VPP

ORIENT
PAPERBACKS

Madarsa Rd, Kashmere Gate
Delhi - 110 006. India